STORIES FROM TH

MAHĀBHĀRATA

PART ONE

A SANSKRIT LANGUAGE COURSE

Seven Sanskrit Coursebooks for Beginners

Pages: viii, 76   Pages: viii, 76   Pages: viii, 60

Pages: xiv, 162   Pages: xv, 189   Pages: xviii, 125   Pages: xiv, 137

All books are A4 Size (297x210 mm) and available in paperback, spiral bound and hardbound.

Extracts from reviews:

The textbooks are reader friendly and enhance the user's creative skills by providing the opportunity to draw and paint alongside stories.

—THE SPEAKING TREE,
February 26th, 2012

I'm simply overwhelmed with joy just looking at these seven coursebooks. ..... Even after following a traditional twelve-year grammar course, the curiosity of Sanskrit lovers is not satiated. ... For such people this *Bhagiratha* (great) attempt is certainly praiseworthy.

—PROF. DAYANANDA BHARGAVA
March 26th, 2012

It is a privilege for me be invited to introduce this set of text books... Only a few students are likely to have the opportunity to go on to study Sanskrit in depth, so that they can enjoy reading Sanskrit by themselves. ..... And the few who go further will be grateful that these books have launched them on an unforgettable experience.

—PROF. RICHARD GOMBRICH
in his 'Preface'

These coursebooks are well-graded, and supported by appropriate illustrations that make them very attractive to learners, particularly the young. Today many Indian and foreign schools/colleges offer Sanskrit as an optional subject. For such students these books are a very effective means of introducing Sanskrit, which they might not have studied previously. These books could also be useful for those involved in performing arts, such as dance and music, or for students of Yoga and Ayurveda—subjects which have many Sanskrit references.

—PROF. SATYAVRAT SHASTRI
in his 'Foreword'

Stories From

The Mahābhārata

A Sanskrit Coursebook for Intermediate Level

Edited by
WARWICK JESSUP
ELENA JESSUP

PART I

MOTILAL BANARSIDASS PUBLISHERS
PRIVATE LIMITED • DELHI

First Edition : Delhi, 2016

Published under arrangements with
St James Schools,
Sanskrit Department, London

ISBN : 978-81-208-4014-0 (PB Part I)
ISBN : 978-81-208-4015-7 (PB Part II)
ISBN : 978-81-208-4016-4 (PB Part III)
ISBN : 978-81-208-4013-3 (Set HB)

MOTILAL BANARSIDASS
41 U.A. Bungalow Road, Jawahar Nagar, Delhi 110 007
8 Mahalaxmi Chamber, 22 Bhulabhai Desai Road, Mumbai 400 026
203 Royapettah High Road, Mylapore, Chennai 600 004
236, 9th Main III Block, Jayanagar, Bengaluru 560 011
Sanas Plaza, 1302 Baji Rao Road, Pune 411 002
8 Camac Street, Kolkata 700 017
Ashok Rajpath, Patna 800 004
Chowk, Varanasi 221 001

The Sanskritpada™, SCcomp™ and Flags2 Sanskrit fonts used in this book are designed and distributed by David Hockley, Oxford (tel. 01844 339944).   © 2003 David Hockley.

COVER DRAWING: The sage Vyāsa dictates the Mahābhārata to Gaṇeśa.

Printed in India
by RP Jain at NAB Printing Unit,
A-44, Naraina Industrial Area, Phase I, New Delhi–110028
and published by JP Jain for Motilal Banarsidass Publishers (P) Ltd,
41 U.A. Bungalow Road, Jawahar Nagar, Delhi-110007

The Editors wish to acknowledge the role played by Annette Morgan and other members of the St James Sanskrit faculty in the preparation of the material for this Sanskrit course, and would also like to thank Mariano de la Torre for the illustrations and Michael Croza-Ross for his unstinting work in designing these volumes.

CONTENTS

Teaching Sanskrit

INTRODUCTION

The Sanskrit language in many parts of the world is a new element in today's education. It is an ideal study for the young because its systematic grammar orders the student's mind. At the same time, Sanskrit literature provides the student with an exciting and profound interaction with a classical culture. Furthermore, because Sanskrit is very close to the source of all Indo-European languages, it helps the student appreciate the underlying structure of language as a whole.

'Stories from the Mahābhārata', a new series of Sanskrit textbooks, presents the epic *'Mahābhārata'* in stories which develop students' knowledge of grammar in a gradual way. It is strongly suggested that students should have completed the preceding section of this course, *'The Story of Rāma' (Parts 1 and 2),* before starting this book.

READING AND WRITING THE DEVANĀGARĪ SCRIPT

Fluent reading and writing of the *devanāgarī* script is essential at this point. If the students are commencing this book after the holidays, you will probably want to spend some time practising reading, writing and dictation exercises.

ORAL AND LISTENING EXERCISES

When teaching this course, it is very useful to have an oral component to each lesson. If students spend all their time doing written work and never speaking the language, their learning will not stick. Similarly, listening exercises (i.e., listening to a story read in Sanskrit and then answering questions about it) help to immerse the student in the 'Sanskrit mindset'. Thus, the exercises given in this book can always be used as oral and listening exercises, and games and competitions are even more effective.

The same is true in learning paradigms. Students should not expect that they will learn their case endings by looking them up. Learning of paradigms should be primarily through recitation in the traditional manner (i.e., by the order of singular, dual and plural for each case). As a supporting method, learning for tests may also be done by looking for patterns of recurring words and similarities with other paradigms. Regular oral and written testing of paradigms is necessary to ensure that they are known accurately and by heart. This applies particularly to the paradigms previously learnt.

Not all the exercises in this book need to be completed: some are optional and should be used according to the teacher's discrimination. It is essential that there be a forward momentum to this study.

SENTENCE ANALYSIS

In Chapter One, a new method of sentence analysis is introduced. Previously, the students have tended to translate each Sanskrit word into English and then rearrange those English words to make a credible English sentence. However, in order to train the students to be able to understand Sanskrit better as a language in its own right, a different method of sentence analysis has been devised.

VOCABULARY

The approach to vocabulary in these books is different from that presented in the earlier textbooks. Some new words in a story are underlined, and their English equivalents will be found at the bottom of the page on which they are working. However, in each chapter there is also a list of new vocabulary words. These should be learned and tested, and could usefully form a component of any end-of-term exam.

Verbs are given a different treatment to that of the earlier course. New verbs are presented in three forms, namely the *dhātu* or root, the First Person singular (i.e., the –ति form) and the indeclinable participle (i.e., the –त्वा form).

Each chapter includes a story. It would be helpful to give a written or oral test on the new vocabulary before starting the story.

NOTES TO TEACHERS

Advice to the teacher is indicated in italics.

The Sanskrit Alphabet and its Pronunciation

अ	a	*as in*	approach		ढ	ḍha	*as in*	godhood*
आ	ā	*as in*	star		ण	ṇa	as in	under*
इ	i	*as in*	if		त	ta	*as in*	table
ई	ī	*as in*	feel		थ	tha	*as in*	anthill
उ	u	*as in*	book		द	da	*as in*	day
ऊ	ū	*as in*	food		ध	dha	*as in*	godhead
ऋ	ṛ		A sound made with the tip of the tongue raised but not quite touching the roof of the mouth (something like the ri in 'ring').		न	na	*as in*	no
					प	pa	*as in*	pure
ए	e	*as in*	say		फ	pha	*as in*	loop-hole
ऐ	ai	*as in*	my		ब	ba	*as in*	baby
ओ	o	*as in*	home		भ	bha	*as in*	abhor
औ	au	*as in*	now		म	ma	*as in*	mother
क	ka	*as in*	kite		य	ya	*as in*	yellow
ख	kha	*as in*	block-head		र	ra	*as in*	rosy*
ग	ga	*as in*	gate		ल	la	*as in*	lady
च	gha	*as in*	log-hut		व	va	*as in*	awake
ङ	ṅa	*as in*	long		श	śa	*as in*	shall
च	ca	*as in*	chalk		ष	ṣa	*as in*	show*
छ	cha	*as in*	catch him		स	sa	*as in*	slug
ज	ja	*as in*	jug		ह	ha	*as in*	heaven
झ	jha	*as in*	hedgehog					
ञ	ña	*as in*	cringe		ं	ṃ		*as in a pure nasal*
ट	ṭa	*as in*	take*		ः	ḥ		*as in an exhaled breath*
ठ	ṭha	*as in*	anthill*					
ड	ḍa	*as in*	do*					

* with the tongue raised to the roof of the mouth

Note to Teachers

In addition to their revision of the grammatical terms described on pages 2–4, students should review, and be tested on, the forms of the following words:

Nouns	Verbs
रामः	भवति
मित्रम्	भविष्यति
सीता	अभवत्
नदी	वर्धते
	अस्ति
	आसीत्

Some related exercises may be found on pages 10 to 20.

Grammatical Terms

NOUN	A **noun** is a person, place or thing.
	e.g. रामः Rāma
	अयोध्या Ayodhyā
	सूत्रम् rope
ADJECTIVE	An **adjective** is a word that describes a noun.
	e.g. पीत॰ yellow
	पाण्डु॰ pale
	The ॰ symbol at the end of these words indicates that they may take endings in three genders, eight cases, and three numbers.
VERB	A **verb** is an action word.
	e.g. पिबति he drinks
	गमिष्यामि I shall go
CASE ENDINGS	The **case ending** of a noun shows the role of that noun in the sentence.
	e.g. रामस्य <u>of</u> Rāma
	सीतया <u>by</u> Sītā
	There are seven cases in Sanskrit plus the vocative:

FIRST CASE ENDING	often the doer
VOCATIVE	the person addressed
SECOND CASE ENDING	the object 'done to'
THIRD CASE ENDING	by or with
FOURTH CASE ENDING	for
FIFTH CASE ENDING	from
SIXTH CASE ENDING	of
SEVENTH CASE ENDING	in (or on)

AGREEMENT	**Agreement** means that adjectives agree in case, number and gender with the nouns they go with.
	e.g. चोरः राक्षसः horrible demon
	चोराय राक्षसाय for the horrible demon
	चोरैः राक्षसैः by horrible demons
NUMBER	The **number** of a word shows whether that word is singular, dual or plural.
	e.g. खगः bird *(singular)*
	खगौ two birds *(dual)*
	खगाः birds *(plural)*
	Note that the plural for 'bird' is simply translated as 'birds', while the dual is translated as 'two birds'.
MASCULINE	A **masculine** word names something considered to be male.
	e.g. रामः Rāma
	हरिः Lord
	गुरुः teacher
FEMININE	A **feminine** word names something considered to be female.
	e.g. सीता Sītā
	नदी river
	मतिः thought
NEUTER	A **neuter** word names something considered to be neither male nor female.
	e.g. मित्रम् friend

TENSE	The **tense** of a verb shows the time in which the action is happening.	

e.g.

खादति	he eats	*(present tense)*
खादिष्यति	he will eat	*(future tense)*
अखादत्	he ate	*(past tense)*

PARADIGM

A **paradigm** (pronounced par-a-dime) is a list or table of all the possible forms that a noun, adjective, pronoun or verb can take.

PERSON

A verb can be expressed in one of three **Persons**. In Sanskrit grammar these are known as:

	SINGULAR	DUAL	PLURAL
First Person	he/she/it	they two	they
Middle Person	you	you two	you
Best Person	I	we two	we

Later languages (for example, Latin and French) deal with these Persons in the opposite order:

	SINGULAR	DUAL	PLURAL
First Person	I	we two	we
Second Person	you	you two	you
Third Person	he/she/it	they two	they

In this course, we shall use the Sanskrit system.

4

CHAPTER ONE

1.1 The Sanskrit Language

Sanskrit is one of the oldest languages in the world. It is the language of the *Vedas, Upaniṣads, Bhagavad Gītā, Mahābhārata, Rāmāyaṇa* and the *Purāṇas*. These books provide an insight into the history of the world and the evolution of humanity. Also, there are books on many other subjects written in Sanskrit. Some of these deal with medicine, astronomy, architecture, mathematics, dance, art and science.

Sanskrit is, or is close to, the mother of all Indo-European languages, including Greek, Latin and English. The word *saṃskṛta* means 'refined language'. This refinement is brought about through its precise grammatical structure which has remained unchanged throughout millennia.

The great grammarian, Pāṇini, explained these laws of grammar in a systematic and beautiful way.

FINDING PĀṆINI ON THE INTERNET

See what is available on the Internet about the great grammarian, Pāṇini. Here is a website to start you off:
http://www.factmonster.com/ce6/people/A0837484.html

Also, try putting 'Pāṇini grammar' into an internet search engine to find interesting and well researched information about Pāṇini's life and work.

1.2 Epic Civilization: Pāṇini

When Pāṇini was a boy, he was not very good in his lessons at school. The other boys used to laugh at him.

"You are a fool," they said.

But Pāṇini, unconcerned, continued to serve his teacher faithfully and always did what he was told. One day, he went for a walk in the mountains by himself. There he remembered the Great Lord, who appeared before him. Pāṇini was amazed.

"Since you have always served and obeyed your teacher, I shall give you whatever you desire," said the Great Lord.

"I desire knowledge," replied Pāṇini.

"Then you will receive a divine grammar," promised the Great Lord.

When Pāṇini returned to his classmates, he challenged them to a grammar competition to see who knew most. The competition went on for eight days. On the eighth day, it seemed that Pāṇini was almost beaten. But at this point, the Great Lord intervened and made Pāṇini victorious.

One key feature of Pāṇini's grammar is his explanation of how words come from dhātus (see page 8).

The Great Lord (Naṭarāja) who appeared to Pāṇini.

1.3 Dhātus

One of the key elements in the Sanskrit language is the system of roots. Words in Sanskrit have at their centre a *dhātu* or root. This is the seed of the word. Thus the *dhátu* खाद् expresses the action of eating; the *dhātu* तुद् expresses the action of hitting; the *dhātu* भू expresses the act of becoming. All the different forms of a Sanskrit verb are formed from its *dhātu*. Nouns and adjectives also come from *dhātus*.

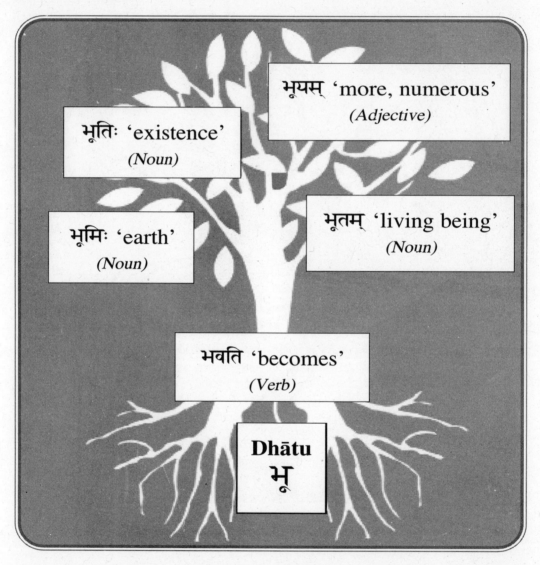

भूयस् 'more, numerous'
(Adjective)

भूतिः 'existence'
(Noun)

भूमिः 'earth'
(Noun)

भूतम् 'living being'
(Noun)

भवति 'becomes'
(Verb)

Dhātu
भू

There are over 2,000 dhātus in Sanskrit,
and from these thousands and thousands of words are formed!

EXERCISE 1

Here are five *dhātus*:

(a) जीव्   (b) चर्   (c) खाद्   (d) वद्   (e) मिल्

in living   in moving   in eating   in speaking   in meeting

Below is a list of five words. State which *dhātu* goes with each word.

For example: अवदत् = (d)

1. खाद्यम् (food)
2. जीवः (a creature)
3. चरित्रम् (behaviour)
4. अमिलत् (he, she or it met)
5. वदान्य॰ (eloquent)

1.4 Stems (The Expansion of *Dhātus*)

There are three stages in the formation of a word:

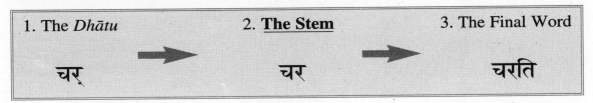

1. The *Dhātu*	2. **The Stem**	3. The Final Word
चर्	चर	चरति

What changes do you notice at each stage?

9

1.5 Verbs

A verb is an action word and can be expressed in the present, past or future tenses. The forms of verbs are called **conjugations**. Here are three examples:

भवति etc. — Present Tense of धातु भू

Singular	Dual	Plural
भवति he, she, it becomes	भवतः they two become	भवन्ति they become
भवसि you become	भवथः you two become	भवथ you become
भवामि I become	भवावः we two become	भवामः we become

भविष्यति etc. — Future Tense of धातु भू

Singular	Dual	Plural
भविष्यति he, she, it will become	भविष्यतः they two will become	भविष्यन्ति they will become
भविष्यसि you will become	भविष्यथः you two will become	भविष्यथ you will become
भविष्यामि I shall become	भविष्यावः we two shall become	भविष्यामः we shall become

अभवत् etc. — Past Tense of धातु भू

Singular	Dual	Plural
अभवत् he, she, it became	अभवताम् they two became	अभवन् they became
अभवः you became	अभवतम् you two became	अभवत you became
अभवम् I became	अभवाव we two became	अभवाम we became

EXERCISE 2

Using the paradigms above, and on page 10, conjugate the following three *dhātus* in the present and past tenses, just writing the Sanskrit (not the English translation):

(a) खाद्   (b) वद्   (c) चर्

EXERCISE 3

Translate the following verbs into English:

1. चरति
2. वदमि
3. जीविष्यामः
4. खादिष्यथ
5. अमिलन्

6. अचरः
7. वदिष्यामि
8. अजीवत्
9. मिलति
10. अखादत्

EXERCISE 4

Translate into Sanskrit:

1. I shall eat
2. they live
3. he says
4. he will meet
5. they walk

6. he became
7. she spoke
8. I became
9. you met
10. they ate

-त्वा WORDS AND *DHĀTUS*

In future, when we are given a new verb it will be expressed in three parts: the *dhātu,* the verb form, and the -त्वा form.
Example:

भू	भवति	भूत्वा
become	he/she/it becomes	having become

EXERCISE 5

(1) Conjugate the following *dhātus* in the future tense, with an English translation:

    (a) खाद्   (b) वद्   (c) चर्

(2) Here are some unusual future forms. Translate them into English. You may need to look at the Sanskrit into English vocabulary in Appendix 4 at the very end of this book.

    (a) गमिष्यति   (d) गमिष्यतः

    (b) गमिष्यन्ति   (e) गमिष्यावः

    (c) द्रक्ष्यामि

12

1.6 Nouns

A noun is a name of a person, place or thing. The forms of nouns are called **declensions.** Here are three examples:

रामः (Rāma): paradigm for masculine nouns ending in अ

Singular	Dual	Plural
रामः Rama	रामौ two Rāmas	रामाः Rāmas
हे राम O Rama	हे रामौ O two Rāmas	हे रामाः O Rāmas
रामम् Rama (2nd)	रामौ two Rāmas (2nd)	रामान् Rāmas (2nd)
रामेण by Rama	रामाभ्याम् by two Rāmas	रामैः by Rāmas
रामाय for Rama	रामाभ्याम् for two Rāmas	रामेभ्यः for Rāmas
रामात् from Rama	रामाभ्याम् from two Rāmas	रामेभ्यः from Rāmas
रामस्य of Rama	रामयोः of two Rāmas	रामाणाम् of Rāmas
रामे in Rama	रामयोः in two Rāmas	रामेषु in Rāmas

मित्रम् ('friend'): paradigm for neuter nouns ending in अ

Singular	Dual	Plural
मित्रम् friend	मित्रे two friends	मित्राणि friends
हे मित्र O friend	हे मित्रे O two friends	हे मित्राणि O friends
मित्रम् friend (2nd)	मित्रे two friends (2nd)	मित्राणि friends (2nd)

The rest of this paradigm is declined like रामः.

सीता (Sītā): paradigm for feminine nouns ending in आ

Singular	Dual	Plural
सीता Sītā	सीते two Sītās	सीताः Sītās
हे सीते O Sītā	हे सीते O two Sītās	हे सीताः O Sītās
सीताम् Sītā (2nd)	सीते two Sītās (2nd)	सीताः Sītās (2nd)
सीतया by Sītā	सीताभ्याम् by two Sītās	सीताभिः by Sītās
सीतायै for Sītā	सीताभ्याम् for two Sītās	सीताभ्यः for Sītās
सीतायाः from Sīta	सीताभ्याम् from two Sītās	सीताभ्यः from Sītās
सीतायाः of Sītā	सीतयोः of two Sītās	सीतानाम् of Sītās
सीतायाम् in Sītā	सीतयोः in two Sītās	सीतासु in Sītās

EXERCISE 6

Using the paradigms of रामः, मित्रम्, and सीता, decline the following words in the singular:

(a) कामः (desire, *masc.*)   (c) गङ्गा (Gaṅgā, *fem.*)

(b) सुखम् (happiness, *neut.*)

EXERCISE 7

Translate the following into English or Sanskrit. Where necessary, use the vocabulary in the Appendices 3 and 4.

1. रामस्य   8. for a man
2. मित्रेषु   9. in desire
3. सीतायै   10. by two boats
4. नगरेभ्यः   11. the houses
5. गङ्गाभिः   12. the two cities
6. गजयोः   13. by elephant
7. कामात्   14. kings (2nd)

15

1.7 Agreement of Doer and Verb

Remember that actions can be done by one doer, two doers or many doers. For example:

खादति   खादतः   खादन्ति

he, she or it eats   two eat   they eat

खगः खादति।   A bird *(singular)* eats.

खगौ खादतः।   Two birds *(dual)* eat.

खगाः खादन्ति।   Birds *(plural)* eat.

Notice in each sentence how **both** the doer and the verb take endings according to whether they speak of one, two or many.

EXERCISE 8

Translate the English word into Sanskrit to form a correct Sanskrit sentence. Then translate the whole sentence into English.

1. नृपः (speaks)।
2. गजाः (walk)।
3. मत्स्यौ (eat)।
4. मित्रे (meet)।
5. कृष्णः (lives)।

16

EXERCISE 9

(a) Choose the correct form from the two in brackets.
(b) Write out the correct Sanskrit sentence.
(c) Translate the sentence into English.

1. (खगः, खगाः) पश्यति।
2. (मित्रे, मित्राणि) अमिलताम्।
3. (नराः, नरौ) सुखेन जीविष्यन्ति।
4. (नृपौ, नृपाः) चरन्ति।
5. (पुस्तकम्, पुस्तके) पततः।

EXERCISE 10

Choose the correct form from the two in brackets and write out the correct Sanskrit sentence. Then translate the sentence.

1. नृपाः सीताम् (गच्छति, गच्छन्ति)।
2. राक्षसाः नगरम् (चरति, चरन्ति)।
3. पुत्रः वनम् (गमिष्यति, गमिष्यन्ति)।
4. बालकस्य सोदरः जलम् (प्रविशति, प्रविशन्ति)।
5. कन्याः गृहात् (अचरत्, अचरन्)।

EXERCISE 11

Translate these sentences. The first few examples may be set out as follows:

The man   walks.
नरः   चरति।

1. The king walks.
2. The friend eats.
3. Two friends walk.
4. Two kings meet.
5. The kings live.

6. The king walked.
7. The friend ate.
8. Two friends walked.
9. Two kings met.
10. The kings lived.

1.8 Feminine Nouns Ending in ई

We shall use the example of नदी (river). Its endings are in some ways similar to those of सीता. Note that देवी (goddess) goes like नदी.

नदी ('river'): paradigm for feminine nouns ending in ई

Singular	Dual	Plural
नदी river	नद्यौ two rivers	नद्यः rivers
हे नदि O river	हे नद्यौ O two rivers	हे नद्यः O rivers
नदीम् river (2nd)	नद्यौ two rivers (2nd)	नदीः rivers (2nd)
नद्या by a river	नदीभ्याम् by two rivers	नदीभिः by rivers
नद्यै for a river	नदीभ्याम् for two rivers	नदीभ्यः for rivers
नद्याः from a river	नदीभ्याम् from two rivers	नदीभ्यः from rivers
नद्याः of a river	नद्योः of two rivers	नदीनाम् of rivers
नद्याम् in a river	नद्योः in two rivers	नदीषु in rivers

EXERCISE 12

Translate into English:

1. नृपाः नदीम् गच्छन्ति।
2. देव्यौ चरतः।
3. नद्याः धावति।
4. देवीम् नमति।
5. देव्यः पिबन्ति।

20

1.9 The Golden Rules of Translation

1 **FIND THE VERB.** After reading a sentence accurately, find the verb, which will usually be at the end of the sentence. Write 'verb' above the verb and then write the English meaning beneath. For example:

verb
नरः   कुक्कुरान्   मार्गे   पश्यति ।
he/she/it sees

2 **FIND THE DOER (Subject)** and then write above it 'doer'. Add the English beneath.

doer   *verb*
नरः   कुक्कुरान्   मार्गे   पश्यति ।
man   *he/she/it sees*

3 **FIND THE OBJECT (The 'Done To')** and then above it put 'object'. Add the English beneath.

doer   *object*   *verb*
नरः   कुक्कुरान्   मार्गे   पश्यति ।
man   *dogs*   *he/she/it sees*

4 **TRANSLATE ANY OTHER WORDS.**

doer   *object*   *verb*
नरः   कुक्कुरान्   मार्गे   पश्यति ।
man   *dogs*   *in road*   *he/she/it sees*

5 Finally, **TRANSLATE THE SENTENCE** directly into English.

The man sees the dogs in the road.

1.10 Vocabulary for Story 1

Note to teacher: Words with an asterisk (*) are part of the IGCSE vocabulary.

NOUNS

*कामः (m)	desire	
*नृपः (m)	king	
*दोषः (m)	fault	
*नदी (f)	river	

*सुखम् (n)	happiness, pleasure	
*भार्या (f)	wife	
*देवी (f)	goddess	
*नारी (f)	lady	

INDECLINABLES (words that do not change their ending) etc.

*नाम	by name		*समीपे	near (+ 6th)
*अतीव	very		*तु	but
*एकदा	once, once upon a time		*सह	together with
*इति	thus		*किम्	what?

DHĀTUS

अस्	in being[1]
जीव्	in living
चर्	in walking
मिल्	in meeting
वद्	in speaking
त्यज्	in leaving
भू	in becoming
कृ	in doing, making
प्रछ्	in asking

VERBS

*अस्ति[2]	he is, there is
*जीवति	he lives
*चरति	he walks
*मिलति (+ 3rd)	he meets
*वदति	he says, speaks
*त्यजति	he leaves
*भवति	he becomes
*करोति	he does, makes
*पृच्छति	he asks

'-त्वा' ENDINGS

जीवित्वा	having lived
चरित्वा	having walked
मिलित्वा	having met
उदित्वा	having spoken
त्यक्ता	having left
भूत्वा	having become
कृत्वा	having done, made
पृष्ट्वा	having asked

[1] *The meaning of a dhātu is traditionally given as being found 'in' an activity.*

[2] *The past tense of अस्ति is आसीत् (he was, there was).*

Gaṅgā, the river goddess

1.11 Story 1

A STRANGE WIFE

King Śāntanu meets the beautiful river goddess Gaṅgā. He immediately falls in love, and pleads with her to be his wife. She consents, but says that if Śāntanu ever asks her what she is doing, she will leave him. A strange wife and a stranger bargain! Can Śāntanu fulfil the strict regulation laid upon him?

1. आसीत् नृपः शान्तनुः नाम।

2. सः अतीव साधुः नृपः सुखेन अजीवत्।

3. तस्य तु एकः दोषः। तस्य दोषः कामः।

4. एकदा शान्तनुः नद्याः समीपे अचरत्।

5. सः नार्या सह अमिलत्।

6. सा नारी देवी गङ्गा नाम। सा अतीव सुन्दरी नारी।

7. मम भार्या भव दयया इति शान्तनुः अवदत्।

[continues on page 26]

Śāntanu meets Gaṅgā.

[continued from page 24]

8. गङ्गा अवदत् <u>अहम्</u> <u>तव</u> भार्या भविष्यामि।

9. किम् <u>करोषि</u> इति <u>न कदापि</u> <u>माम्</u> पृच्छ।

10. <u>यदि</u> तत् पृच्छसि <u>तर्हि</u> <u>त्वाम्</u> त्यजामि इति॥

शान्तनुः	Śāntanu, a great king	अहम्	I *(see page 148)*
सः / सा	he / she *(see pages 143 / 144)*	तव	your, of you *(6th sg. of त्वम्)*
सुखेन	happily	करोषि	you do
तस्य	his, of him *(see page 143)*	न कदापि	never
गङ्गा	Gaṅgā, the river goddess	माम्	me (2nd) *(see page 148)*
मम	my, of me *(see page 148)*	पृच्छ	ask!
भव	be!	यदि . . . तर्हि	if . . . then . . .
दयया	please	त्वाम्	you *(2nd sg. of त्वम्)*

1.12 Sanskrit Crossword Puzzle No. 1

Note: Some of the answers require more than one word. Where this is the case, the numerals shown in brackets (immediately following the clue) refer to the number of letters in each word of the answer.

Across

1. Translate: *samīpe*.

5. Translate: *doṣa*.

11. What are these pairs called (p.30): *yadā ... tadā ...; yatra ... tatra ...?*

13. What does *iṣya* indicate in a Sanskrit verb?

15. How many lines of words are there in a noun paradigm?

16. Which gender do these endings fall under: *yā, yai, yāḥ, yāḥ, yām?*

17. What does the ending *ena* mean? Give two possibilities. (2, 4)

20. What is the basic Sanskrit word order in a sentence? (7, 6, 4)(p.21)

23. What is the writing of Sanskrit letters in English letters called? (p.127)

25. Translate: *asmi*. (1,2) (p. 132)

27. Translate: *tyaktvā*. (6, 4)

28. Where would you usually find the verb in a Sanskrit sentence?

31. For which English verb does Sanskrit have no word? (p. 91)

32. Who is Rāma's wife?

33. Translate: *devī*.

34. Which case in a noun paradigm gives the <u>object</u> endings?

35. Translate: *agacchāma* (2, 4)

Down

1. Endings showing a doer agree with verbal endings in ....

28

2. Translate: *nārī*.

3. The first word is 'he'. (2, 4)

4. Which case in a noun paradigm often shows the doer?

6. Translate: *bhaviṣyanti*. (4, 4, 6)

7. With which case are the verbs *namati* (he bows) and *dadāti* (he gives) used? (See pp. 166 and 167)

8. Translate: *naram gatvā*. (6, 4, 2, 3, 3)

9. By the side of what did *Śāntanu* meet *Gaṅgā*?

10. Who was *Śāntanu*?

12. Which case is used with the word *samīpe*? (See p. 22)

14. What do present and future tense verbs share in common?

18. How many basic tenses are there for a verb?

19. What are the three stages in forming a word? (4, 4, 4) The first stage is 'root' (see p. 9).

21. Which case is used to express the verb *has, have, had*? (see p. 91)

22. Who was *Gaṅgā*?

23. What case is always used with the verb *milati*? (see p. 169)

24. Translate 'Run!'(imperative singular)

26. Translate: 'two sages' (see p. 137).

29. What is the root of the verb *khādati*?

30. Translate: *kāma*.

CHAPTER TWO

2.1 Epic Civilization: Rivers

Rivers are important because they provide something essential for life — water. So towns and cities have normally been built where there is a river. Since the water flows all the time and is ever-fresh, rivers keep everything clean.

Sanskrit literature often speaks of rivers as goddesses. Gaṅgā is an example of a river goddess. Gaṅgā is the river Ganges. It is one of the largest rivers in the world. Its source is found among the tallest mountains in the world, the Himālayas (Sanskrit for 'home of the snows').

The River Gaṅgā descending from the Himālayas.

2.2 Complementary Sentences

We now look at a sentence with two sides that complement, or complete, each other. For example:

यत्र यत्र नदी अस्ति तत्र तत्र जलम् अस्ति।
Wherever there is a river, there is water.

यत्र यत्र नदी अस्ति }   { तत्र तत्र जलम् अस्ति

Above are the two halves of the sentence. Can you see that they work together? This is an example of the यत्र यत्र ... तत्र तत्र type of complementary sentence — just one of the complements listed below.

COMPLEMENTS

*यत्र ... तत्र	where . . . there
*यत्र यत्र ... तत्र तत्र	wherever . . . there
*यदा ... तदा	when . . . then
*यदा यदा ... तदा तदा	whenever . . . then
*यदि ... तर्हि	if . . . then
*यः ... सः	he who . . . he
*यथा ... तथा	as . . . so
*यावत् ... तावत्	as long as . . . for so long

ADVERBIAL ENDINGS

'–दा'   indicates 'time'   e.g., यदा = when

'–त्र'   indicates 'place'   e.g., यत्र = where

'–था'   indicates 'manner'   e.g., यथा = as

30

EXERCISE 13

Translate into English:

1.

| यत्र नृपः वसति | तत्र भार्या वसति। |

2.

| यदा देवी वदति | तदा नरः सुखितः भवति। |

3.

| यत्र यत्र नरः गच्छति | तत्र तत्र कुक्कुरः अनुगच्छति। |

4.

| यथा जनः चिन्तयति | तथा सः भविष्यति। |

5.

| यदि नारी खगम् शृणोति | तर्हि सा हसति। |

6.

| यः अग्नौ तिष्ठति | सः दग्धः भविष्यति। |

7.

| यावत् नरः साधुः अस्ति | तावत् सुखितः भविष्यति। |

EXERCISE 14

Translate the following into English:

1. यत्र देवी आगच्छति तत्र राक्षसाः तस्याः धावन्ति।
2. यदा रामः सीताम् अपश्यत् तदा सः सुखितः अभवत्।
3. यः प्रबलः सः राक्षसान् जयति।
4. यदि शान्तनुः पृच्छति किम् करोषि इति तर्हि गङ्गा तम् त्यजति।

EXERCISE 15

Translate into Sanskrit:

1. When the boy meets the demon, then they will do battle.

2. As Sītā thinks so she will do.

3. If I meet my friend here, then we shall walk to the mountain.

4. Wherever Rāma goes, he conquers demons.

2.3 The Second Case Ending

The second case ending indicates the object — the person or thing — affected by the action. Here are some examples.

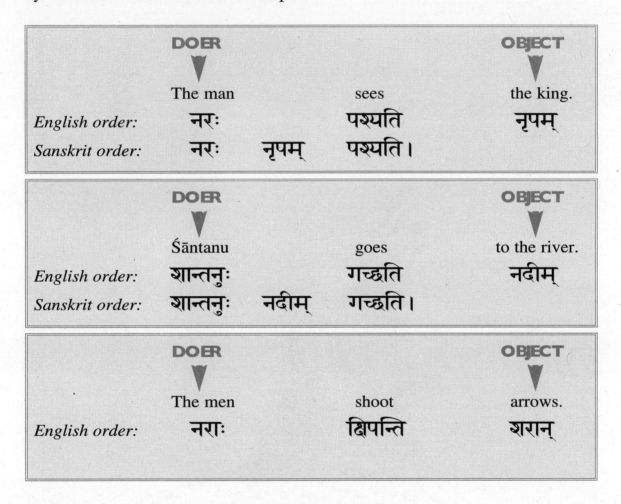

Notice how in the <u>Sanskrit</u> order of a completed sentence the verb is at the end and is followed by a sign called a विराम or 'stop'. Also, notice how the doer and the verb agree.

EXERCISE 16

Translate into English or Sanskrit. Use the 'Sanskrit order' method shown above.

1. शान्तनुः जलम् पिबति।
2. नृपः फले खादति।
3. नारी दोषान् पश्यति।
4. The wise kings walked to the strong man.
5. The good son went home quickly.

King Śāntanu

2.4 The Paradigm of हरिः

हरिः (Lord) is a masculine word. This paradigm gives the pattern for masculine nouns ending in इ.

हरिः ('Lord'): paradigm for masculine nouns ending in इ

Singular	*Dual*	*Plural*
हरिः Lord	हरी two Lords	हरयः Lords
हे हरे O Lord	हे हरी O two Lords	हे हरयः O Lords
हरिम् Lord (2nd)	हरी two Lords (2nd)	हरीन् Lords (2nd)
हरिणा * by the Lord	हरिभ्याम् by two Lords	हरिभिः by Lords
हरये for the Lord	हरिभ्याम् for two Lords	हरिभ्यः for Lords
हरेः from the Lord	हरिभ्याम् from two Lords	हरिभ्यः from Lords
हरेः of the Lord	हर्योः of two Lords	हरीणाम् * of Lords
हरौ in the Lord	हर्योः in two Lords	हरिषु in Lords

* Note that in these forms the preceding र् causes न् to change to ण्.

Other words that go like हरिः

कपिः	monkey	मुनिः	sage
ऋषिः	sage	अग्निः	fire

EXERCISE 17

Translate into English:

1. ऋषेः
2. हरिभ्याम्
3. मुनीनाम्
4. अग्नौ
5. कपयः

Translate into Sanskrit:

6. two monkeys (2nd)
7. in a sage
8. for two lords
9. from a monkey
10. O many lords

Gaṅgā consents to marry Śāntanu — but with conditions.

2.5 Vocabulary for Story 2

Note to teacher: Words with an asterisk (*) are part of the IGCSE vocabulary.

PRONOUNS	* सः (m)	he / that	* सा (f)	she / that
	* तत् (n)	that	* किम् (n)	what?

ADJECTIVES	* मृत॰	dead	* अष्टम॰	eighth
	* सप्त	seven		

INDECLINABLES	* अचिरेण	soon	* एवम्	thus
	* इदानीम्	now		

DHĀTUS		**VERBS**		**'-त्वा' ENDINGS**	
क्षिप्	in throwing / shooting	* क्षिपति	he throws / shoots	क्षिप्त्वा	having thrown / shot
दृश् (पश्य)[1]	in seeing	* पश्यति	he sees	दृष्ट्वा	having seen
भू	in being, becoming	* भवति	he becomes	भूत्वा	having become
नी	in leading	* नयति	he leads	नीत्वा	having led
प्रछ्	in asking	* पृच्छति	he asks	पृष्ट्वा	having asked
गम्	in going	* गच्छति	he goes	गत्वा	having gone
आ + गम्	in coming	* आगच्छति	he comes	आगम्य[2]	having come

[1] दृश् *is an irregular dhātu and the stem is* पश्य.

[2] *Notice the* -य *ending instead of* -त्वा.

GAṄGĀ KILLS THE SONS OF ŚĀNTANU

King Śāntanu marries Gaṅgā and they have seven children. Gaṅgā drowns every child born to her. Little does Śāntanu know that these seven children are gods who have been cursed to be born into human bodies but by special dispensation are allowed to escape from their human bodies shortly after birth. When Gaṅgā is about to drown her eighth child, Śāntanu asks her what she is doing. Gaṅgā leaves him, taking her eighth child with her.

1. शान्तनुः गङ्गाम् पर्यणयत् ।

2. अचिरेण गङ्गायाः पुत्रः आसीत् ।

3. सा तु पुत्रम् नद्याम् अक्षिपत् ।

4. शान्तनुः तत् अपश्यत् ।

5. एवम् गङ्गा सप्त पुत्रान् नद्याम् अक्षिपत् ।

6. ते सर्वे मृताः अभवन् ।

[continues on page 40]

Gaṅgā leaves Śāntanu, taking her eighth child with her.

[continued from page 38]

7. अचिरेण गङ्गायाः अष्टमः पुत्रः आसीत्।

8. सा पुत्रम् नदीम् अनयत्।

9. शान्तनुः तु किम् <u>करोषि</u> इति अपृच्छत्।

10. गङ्गा अवदत् इदानीम् <u>त्वाम्</u> त्यजामि।

11. तव अष्टमः पुत्रः <u>मया</u> सह आगमिष्यति इति॥

पर्यणयत्	he married	त्वाम्	you (2nd sg.)
करोषि	you do	मया	*(see page 148)*

CHAPTER THREE

3.1 Epic Civilization: Kāma (Desire)

The Sanskrit epics are full of stories in which characters face tests. A common test is whether they will follow their own personal desire, or their duty. The epics teach that कामः (desire) is natural, but needs to come under the regulation of धर्मः (duty).

According to one view, it is King Śāntanu's inability to do this which leads to great trouble. As we shall see in the story at the end of this chapter, his all-consuming desire for the beautiful Satyavatī sets off a chain of unfortunate events. Śāntanu had given his word that his first son, Bhīṣma, would be king. His duty was to honour his word, but he allowed desire to override this, with the result that Bhīṣma had to vow not to be king so that his father could marry Satyavatī.

Bhīṣma

3.2 The Paradigm of गुरुः

गुरुः ('teacher') gives the pattern for masculine nouns ending in उ.

Singular	Dual	Plural
गुरुः teacher	गुरू two teachers	गुरवः teachers
हे गुरो O teacher	हे गुरू O two teachers	हे गुरवः O teachers
गुरुम् teacher (2nd)	गुरू two teachers (2nd)	गुरून् teachers (2nd)
गुरुणा* by the teacher	गुरुभ्याम् by two teachers	गुरुभिः by teachers
गुरवे for the teacher	गुरुभ्याम् for two teachers	गुरुभ्यः for teachers
गुरोः from the teacher	गुरुभ्याम् from two teachers	गुरुभ्यः from teachers
गुरोः of the teacher	गुर्वोः of two teachers	गुरुणाम्* of teachers
गुरौ in the teacher	गुर्वोः in two teachers	गुरुषु in teachers

Note that in these forms the preceding र causes न to change to ण.

Other masculine words that go like गुरुः

शान्तनुः	Śāntanu	बहु°	much, many
वायुः	wind	पशुः	beast

42

EXERCISE 18

Translate into English:

1. गुरवः
2. पशून्
3. शान्तनवे
4. वायोः
5. बहुना

Translate into Sanskrit:

6. of many (pl.) teachers
7. of two teachers
8. in many teachers
9. by Śāntanu
10. from the wind

43

3.3 The Third Case Ending

The third case ending is used to show the instrument, the thing you might use to do the action. For example:

				Third Case Ending
	The man	eats	fruit	with his hand.
English order:	(नरः	खादति	फलम्	हस्तेन।)
Sanskrit order:	नरः	फलम्	हस्तेन	खादति।

EXERCISE 19

Translate into Sanskrit, using the method shown above. Do not forget to put the verb last!

1. The man goes to town by chariot.
2. The goddess goes to the forest by boat.
3. The demoness meets with her son.
4. The two monkeys eat fruits with their hands.
5. The king came to the river with the sage.

44

3.4 Words ending in -त

A -त ending word has the sense of a completed action. Like an adjective, its ending is modified in case, number and gender so that it agrees with the noun it describes. In English grammar we call a -त ending word a 'past passive participle' (ppp). For example, रामः गतः। 'Rāma (has) gone.' Here is a list of some -त words:

DHĀTUS	-त ENDING WORDS	MEANING
कृ	*कृत॰	made / done
गम्	*गत॰	gone
आ + गम्	आगत॰	come
मृ	*मृत॰	dead
हन्	*हत॰	killed / struck
श्रु	श्रुत॰	heard / listened to
दृश्[1]	*दृष्ट॰	seen
खाद्	खादित॰	eaten
अप + हृ	अपहृत॰	carried off
ग्रह्[1]	*गृहीत॰	grabbed / seized
वच्[1]	*उक्त॰	said / spoken
पत्	पतित॰	fallen

1 Has irregular forms.
* Indicates IGCSE vocabulary.

EXERCISE 20

Translate the following into English. 'Has', 'was' or 'has/have been' will need to be supplied in the translation.

1. भीष्मः गतः ।
2. फलम् खादितम् ।
3. कन्या अपहृता ।
4. कपी दृष्टौ ।
5. गुरवः श्रुताः ।

EXERCISE 21

Translate into Sanskrit using –त ending words. The bracketed words in the following sentences do not get translated into Sanskrit:

1. The desire (has) gone.
2. The marriage (was) made by the sage.
3. The dead king (had) fallen to the ground.
4. The demoness (was) seen by him.
5. The wind (was) heard in the trees.

3.5 The Paradigms of तत्, सः and सा

A pronoun is used instead of a noun to designate a person, place or thing. For example, तत्, सः and सा.

The paradigm of the **neuter** pronoun तत् ('that'):

Singular	Dual	Plural
तत् that	ते those two	तानि those
तत् that (2nd)	ते those two (2nd)	तानि those (2nd)
तेन by that	ताभ्याम् by those two	तैः by those
तस्मै for that	ताभ्याम् for those two	तेभ्यः for those
तस्मात् from that	ताभ्याम् from those two	तेभ्यः from those
तस्य of that	तयोः of those two	तेषाम् of those
तस्मिन् in that	तयोः in those two	तेषु in those

The paradigm of the **masculine** pronoun सः ('he' / 'that'):

Singular	Dual	Plural
सः he / that	तौ those two	ते those
तम् him / that (2nd)	तौ those two (2nd)	तान् those / them (2nd)

The rest go like तत्,

The paradigm of the **feminine** pronoun सा ('she' / 'that'):

Singular	Dual	Plural
सा she / that	ते those two	ताः those
ताम् her / that (2nd)	ते those two (2nd)	ताः those / them (2nd)
तया by her / that	ताभ्याम् by those two	ताभिः by those
तस्यै for her / that	ताभ्याम् for those two	ताभ्यः for those
तस्याः from her / that	ताभ्याम् from those two	ताभ्यः from those
तस्याः of her / that	तयोः of those two	तासाम् of those
तस्याम् in her / that	तयोः in those two	तासु in those

EXERCISE 22

Translate into English:

1. तया
2. तैः
3. तयोः
4. तासु
5. तत्

EXERCISE 23

Translate into Sanskrit.

1. he
2. she
3. for him
4. for her
5. by those two (neuter)

EXERCISE 24

Translate into English:

1. सः कपिः
2. सा देवी
3. तत् मित्रम्
4. तस्मिन् वने
5. ताभ्याम् गुरुभ्याम्

EXERCISE 25

Choose the correct form from the three in brackets and write out the correct Sanskrit phrase. Then translate the phrase.

1. (तत्, सः, सा) कामः
2. (तस्मिन्, तानि, तस्याम्) दोषे
3. (तेन, तया, तैः) राक्षस्या
4. (तस्मात्, ताः, तस्याः) कपेः
5. (ते, ताः, सा) नारी

EXERCISE 26

Translate into Sanskrit.

1. that monkey
2. from those rivers
3. in that heart
4. by those two friends
5. of that tree

EXERCISE 27

Translate into English:

1. सः नरः ताम् नारीम् अपश्यत्।
2. तेन मुनिना सा तारका दृष्टा।
3. ताः नार्यः तम् नृपम् अनमन्।

50

The paradigms of तत्, सः and सा set the pattern for the declensions of many other pronouns, such as सर्वम्, अन्यत् and एतत् for which the First Case singular endings are given below.

NEUTER	MASCULINE	FEMININE	
सर्वम्	सर्वः	सर्वा	all
अन्यत्	अन्यः	अन्या	other / another
एतत्	एषः	एषा	this

EXERCISE 28

Translate into English:

1. अन्यः देवः
2. एषः दोषः
3. सर्वेषु कामेषु
4. एतस्यै राक्षस्यै
5. सर्वाणि मित्राणि

EXERCISE 29

1. Decline एतत् in the masculine, beginning with एषः, एतौ, एते.
2. Decline सर्वम् in the feminine, beginning with सर्वा, सर्वे, सर्वाः.
3. Decline अन्यत् in the neuter, beginning with अन्यत्, अन्ये, अन्यानि.

EXERCISE 30

Translate these sentences into Sanskrit, following this example:

	The man	walks	to the river.
English order:	नरः	चरति	नदीम् ।
Sanskrit order:	नरः	नदीम् चरति ।	

1. These two boys run.
2. This lion led the deer to the water.
3. The dead bird fell from another tree.
4. Rāma will eat all the fruits.
5. Having seen* the lion, another man ran from the forest.

*Note: You can find 'having seen' under 'seen' in Appendix 3.

3.6 Vocabulary for Story 3

*Note to teacher: Words with an asterisk (*) are part of the IGCSE vocabulary.*

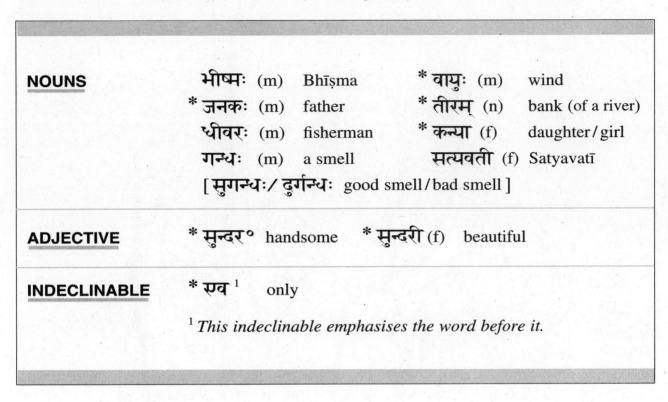

NOUNS	भीष्मः (m)	Bhīṣma	* वायुः (m)	wind
	* जनकः (m)	father	* तीरम् (n)	bank (of a river)
	धीवरः (m)	fisherman	* कन्या (f)	daughter / girl
	गन्धः (m)	a smell	सत्यवती (f)	Satyavatī
	[सुगन्धः / दुर्गन्धः: good smell / bad smell]			

ADJECTIVE	* सुन्दर° handsome	* सुन्दरी (f) beautiful

INDECLINABLE	* एव [1] only

[1] *This indeclinable emphasises the word before it.*

Note to teachers: Here introduce to the students the concept of a family tree.
The tree will be developed later in the book as the story proceeds.

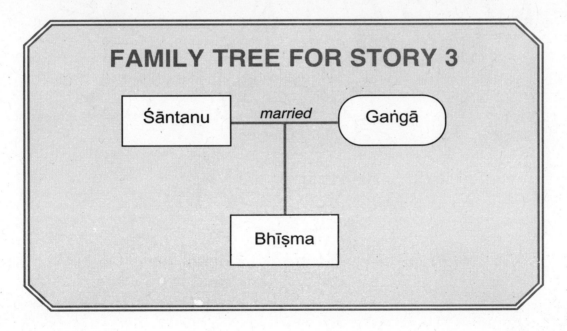

FAMILY TREE FOR STORY 3

Śāntanu —— *married* —— Gaṅgā

Bhīṣma

A couple in their marriage ceremony walk round the sacred fire.

3.7   Story 3

THE FISHERMAN KING'S DAUGHTER

King Śāntanu's eighth son, Bhīṣma, now grown up, returns to his father. Śāntanu proclaims that Bhīṣma will be his heir. One day, while walking by the river, Śāntanu smells a beautiful fragrance. The fragrance leads him to Satyavatī, the dazzling daughter of the king of the fishermen. Will Śāntanu find love once again?

1. शान्तनोः अष्टमः पुत्रः भीष्मः नाम।

2. एकदा भीष्मः शान्तनुम् आगच्छत्।

3. *त्वम्* एव नृपः भविष्यसि इति शान्तनुः भीष्मम् अवदत्।

4. एकदा तु शान्तनुः नद्याः तीरे अचरत्।

5. वायौ सुगन्धः आसीत्।

6. सः सुगन्धः सुन्दर्याः कन्यायाः आगच्छत्।

[continues on page 57]

55

Śāntanu asks Satyavatī's father for her hand in marriage.

[continued from page 55]

7. यत्र यत्र सा नारी अगच्छत् तत्र तत्र सुगन्धः आसीत्।

8. कन्याम् दृष्ट्वा का त्वम् इति शान्तनुः अपृच्छत्।

9. कन्या अवदत् अहम् सत्यवती नाम।

10. मम जनकः धीवराणाम् नृपः अस्ति इति॥

त्वम्	you	अहम्	I
का	who?	मम	my

CHAPTER FOUR

4.1 Epic Civilization: Vows

A vow is when you give your word that you will do something. Once you have given your word, you cannot go back on it.

In Story 4 at the end of this chapter, Bhīṣma, for his father's sake, gave his word to the king of the fishermen that he would give up his claim to the throne. This, Bhīṣma thought, would enable his father to marry Satyavatī, the daughter of the king of the fishermen.

But the king of the fishermen was still not satisfied. He thought that Bhīṣma's sons would claim the throne as their own in the future. So Bhīṣma took another vow that he would never marry or have children.

Bhīṣma kept his word throughout his life.

4.2 Question Words

In English certain words are used at the beginning of a sentence to ask a question. These words are:

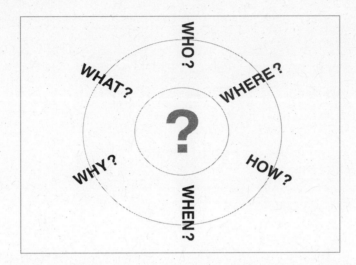

Sanskrit uses question words too, and they always begin with the letter ' क '. For example:

*कुत्र	where?
*कथम्	how?
*कदा	when?

Notice in these words the **adverbial endings**:

-दा	indicating	'time',	e.g., कदा =	when?
-त्र	indicating	'place',	e.g., कुत्र =	where?
-थम्	indicating	'manner',	e.g., कथम् =	how?

Here are some examples of how these question words are used:

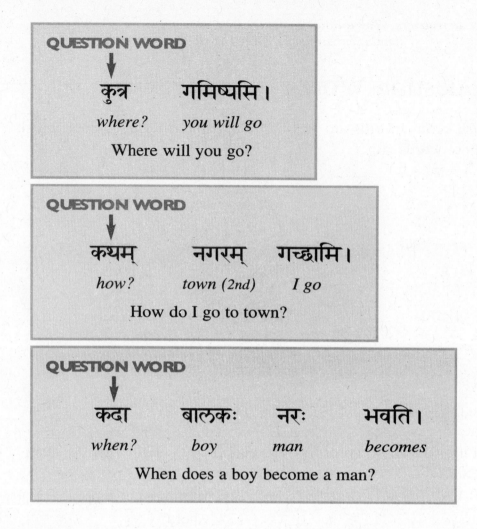

EXERCISE 31

Translate into English. Do not forget to put a question mark at the end of your English sentence.

1. कुत्र सुगन्धः।
2. कदा कामः नरम् त्यजति।
3. कथम् गृहम् गमिष्यामि।
4. कदा नराः वनम् गच्छन्ति।
5. कुत्र राक्षसाः वसन्ति।

QUESTION GAME

Make up three questions in Sanskrit, using the three question words you have just learned. Then, exchange your questions with a neighbour and see if you can answer your neighbour in Sanskrit.

Note to teachers: The following section 4.3 is new material.

4.3 More Question Words

किम् , कः and का are declined in a similar manner to तत् , सः and सा.

The paradigm of the **neuter** pronoun किम् ('what? / 'which?'):

Singular	Dual	Plural
किम् what?	के which two?	कानि which?
किम् what? (2nd)	के which two? (2nd)	कानि which? (2nd)
केन by what?	काभ्याम् by which two?	कैः by which?
कस्मै for what?	काभ्याम् for which two?	केभ्यः for which?
कस्मात् from what?	काभ्याम् from which two?	केभ्यः from which?
कस्य of what?	कयोः of which two?	केषाम् of which?
कस्मिन् in what?	कयोः in which two?	केषु in which?

61

The paradigm of the **masculine** pronoun कः ('who?' / 'what?'):

Singular	Dual	Plural
कः who? / what?	कौ which two?	के which?
कम् whom? / what?	कौ which two (2nd)	कान् which? (2nd)

The paradigm of the **feminine** pronoun का ('who?' / 'what?'):

Singular	Dual	Plural
का who? / what?	के which two?	काः which?
काम् whom? / what?	के which two? (2nd)	काः which? (2nd)
कया by whom? / what?	काभ्याम् by which two?	काभिः by which?
कस्यै for whom? / what?	काभ्याम् for which two?	काभ्यः for which?
कस्याः from whom? / what?	काभ्याम् from which two?	काभ्यः from which?
कस्याः of whom? / what?	कयोः of which two?	कासाम् of which?
कस्याम् in whom? / what?	कयोः in which two?	कासु in which?

EXERCISE 32

Translate into English:

1. काभ्याम्
2. केषाम्
3. के
4. कान्
5. केन

EXERCISE 33

Choose the correct form from the two in brackets and write out the correct Sanskrit phrase. Then translate the phrase.

1. कः (नरः, नारी)
2. का (भूमिः, कपिः)
3. किम् (वनानि, वनम्)
4. काः (देवी, देव्यः)
5. कौ (पुत्रौ, कन्या)
6. कस्मिन् (चन्द्रान्, चन्द्रे)
7. कासाम् (नारीम्, नारीणाम्)
8. के (मित्रे, नरे)
9. कया (नौकायाः, नौकया)
10. कस्मै (कुक्कुरैः, कपये)

EXERCISE 34

Translate into English:

1. कः नरः वदति।
2. के देव्यौ गृहम् अत्यजताम्।
3. केन मार्गेन जनकः आगच्छत्।
4. किम् तव नाम।
5. कस्याः नद्याः धीवराः अचरन्।

EXERCISE 35

Translate into Sanskrit:

1. What is that good smell?
2. Where is that snake?
3. From which monkey does that bad smell come?

Note to teachers: The following material extends a methodical approach to translation from English to Sanskrit.

4.4 The Fourth Case Ending

The Fourth Case Ending shows for whom the action is done. It is also used when a person is given something. For example:

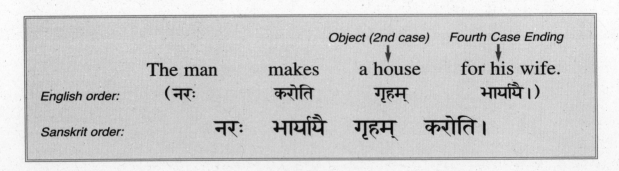

64

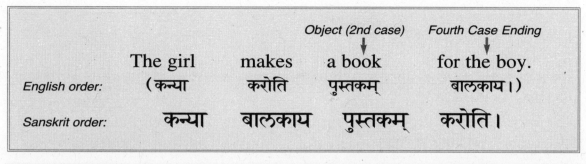

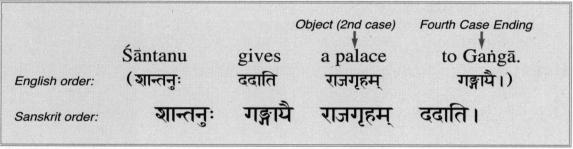

Notice that the person who receives the gift has a fourth case ending and that the thing given is in the second case.

EXERCISE 36

Translate into Sanskrit:

1. The man makes a book for the lady.
2. The man makes a book for two ladies.
3. The man makes a book for the ladies.
4. The demon gives a dead bird to the demoness.
5. The sage gives the son to the man.

4.5 The Use of स्म

The word स्म is used after a verb in the present tense to change that verb into the past. For example:

चिन्तयति स्म   'he thought'

पिबसि स्म   'you drank'

EXERCISE 37

Translate into English:

1. सिंहाः नदीम् चरन्ति स्म।
2. राक्षसः राक्षसीम् नमति स्म।
3. भार्याः ऋषिम् पश्यन्ति स्म।
4. सत्यवती शान्तनुम् वदति स्म।
5. नृपः राजगृहम् रथेन गच्छति स्म।

4.6 Vocabulary for Story 4

Note to teacher: Words with an asterisk (*) are part of the IGCSE vocabulary.

NOUNS	विवाहः (m)	marriage	व्रतम् (n)	vow
	*राजगृहम् (n)	palace		

INDECLINABLES	दुःखेन	unhappily	*पुरा	long ago

DHĀTUS		**VERBS**		**'-त्वा' ENDINGS**	
इष्	in desiring / wanting	*इच्छति	he desires/wants	इष्ट्वा	having desired / wanted
श्रु	in hearing	*शृणोति	he hears	*श्रुत्वा	having heard
(प्रति +) वद्	in replying	*प्रतिवदति	he replies	प्रत्युद्य[1]	having replied
(परि +) नी	in marrying	*परिणयति[2]	he marries	परिणीय[1]	having married

[1] *Notice the* य *ending instead of* -त्वा.
[2] *Notice the* न *becomes a* ण *after a* र.

Note to teachers: The diagram below begins to develop the family tree shown on page 53.

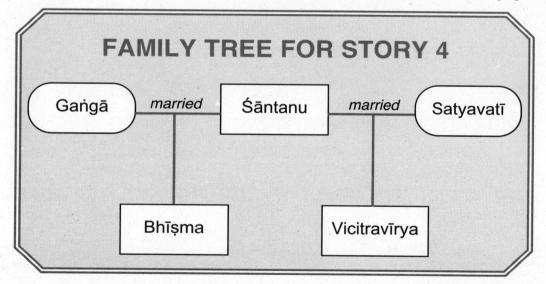

FAMILY TREE FOR STORY 4

Gaṅgā — *married* — Śāntanu — *married* — Satyavatī

Bhīṣma

Vicitravīrya

67

4.7 Story 4

> # Bhīṣma's Vow
>
> Śāntanu asks the king of the fishermen for permission to marry Satyavatī. The king will only consent to the marriage if Śāntanu promises that Satyavatī's son will be the next king. Bhīṣma, for his father's sake, vows that he will give up his claim to the throne and will never marry nor have any children.

1. धीवराणाम् नृपम् गत्वा शान्तनुः वदति स्म।

2. <u>तव</u> कन्याम् विवाहे इच्छामि इति।

3. धीवराणाम् नृपः प्रतिवदति स्म यदि सत्यवती <u>तव</u> भार्या भविष्यति

   तर्हि तस्याः पुत्रः नृपः भविष्यति इति।

4. शान्तनुः राजगृहम् दुःखेन पुनः अगच्छत्।

5. भीष्मः सर्वम् श्रुत्वा धीवराणाम् नृपम् गत्वा <u>तम</u> वदति स्म।

6. पुरा शान्तनुः <u>माम</u> अवदत् हे भीष्म <u>त्वम</u> नृपः भविष्यसि इति।

[continues on page 70]

Bhīṣma making his vow.

[continued from page 68]

7. इदानीम् तु सत्यवत्याः पुत्रः नृपः भविष्यति।

8. <u>अहम्</u> नृपः न भविष्यामि इति <u>मम</u> व्रतम् इति।

9. शान्तनुः सत्यवतीम् परिणयति स्म॥

तव	your	त्वम्	you
तम्	him	अहम्	I
माम्	me	मम	my

CHAPTER FIVE

5.1   Epic Civilization: The Svayaṃvara

The *svayaṃvara* is a ceremony in which a princess can choose a husband.

The king sends out invitations all over the world to eligible young princes to come to the ceremony. When they arrive, their names are read out. There is often a competition in which the princes can show their prowess in archery or other martial arts.

At the end of the competition those seeking the hand of the king's daughter gather before the princess and she puts a garland around the neck of the man she chooses (usually the winner of the competition).

As you will see in Story 5, in Bhīṣma's case he picked up the princesses and put them on his chariot!

A princess makes her choice at a svayaṃvara.

5.2 Indefinites

An indefinite is a word like:

- 'somebody'   (no definite person)
- 'something' (no definite thing)
- 'somewhere' (no definite place)
- 'sometime'   (no definite time)
- 'somehow'   (no definite manner)

In Sanskrit, indefinite words are made by adding चित्, चन and अपि after a
question word. If न is added before the indefinite, you get a negative indefinite, like the words 'no one', 'nothing', 'nowhere', 'never' and 'no way'. For
example:

QUESTION WORD	INDEFINITE	NEGATIVE INDEFINITE
कुत्र where?	कुत्र अपि कुत्र चित् somewhere	न कुत्र अपि न कुत्र चित् nowhere
कथम् how?	कथम् अपि somehow	न कथम् अपि (in) no way
कदा when?	कदा चित् कदा अपि sometimes	न कदा चित् न कदा अपि never
कः / का who? who? (m.) (f.)	कः चन someone *(m.)* का चन someone *(f.)*	न कः चन no-one *(m.)* न का चन no-one *(f.)*

EXERCISE 38

Translate the following sentences into English:

1. अहम् नगरम् कथम् अपि गच्छामि।
2. बालकः कुक्कुरम् न कुत्र चित् अपश्यत्।
3. गुरवः न कदा अपि माम् पृच्छन्ति।
4. त्वम् अश्वम् कुत्र चित् अत्यजः।
5. कुक्कुरः कथम् अपि गृहम् अत्यजत् इति शिष्यः अवदत्।
6. अर्जुनः शरम् कुत्र अपि अक्षिपत्।
7. सुन्दरी कन्या कृष्णस्य शब्दम् न कदा चित् अशृणोत्।
8. कन्याः पुष्पाणि कदा अपि इच्छन्ति।

5.3 The Fifth Case Ending

The Fifth Case Ending shows where an action comes from. For example:

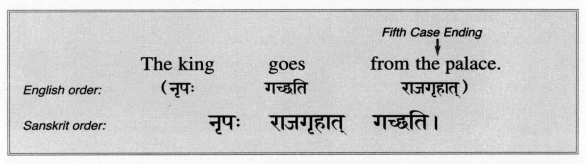

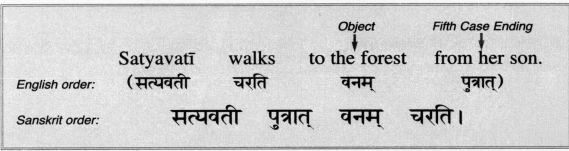

The monkeys | ran | from the fire.

English order: (कपयः | अधावन् | अग्नेः)

Sanskrit order: कपयः | अग्नेः | अधावन् ।

EXERCISE 39

Translate into Sanskrit:

1. The man goes from the house to the forest.
2. Run from the town, son!
3. The wind came from the forest.
4. The demon eats from the tree.
5. The fisherman drank water from the river.

Note to teachers: This further develops the family tree shown on page 67.

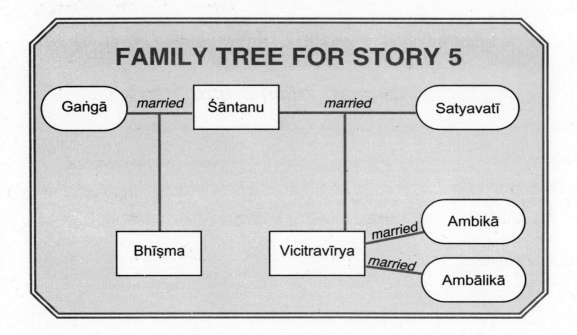

FAMILY TREE FOR STORY 5

Gaṅgā — married — Śāntanu — married — Satyavatī

Bhīṣma

Vicitravīrya — married — Ambikā

Vicitravīrya — married — Ambālikā

5.4 Vocabulary for Story 5

Note to teacher: Words with an asterisk (*) are part of the IGCSE vocabulary.

NOUNS

विचित्रवीर्यः	(m)	Vicitravīrya	अम्बा (f)	Ambā
युवराजः	(m)	heir apparent	अम्बिका (f)	Ambikā
*राजपुत्रः	(m)	prince	अम्बालिका (f)	Ambālikā
स्वयंवरः	(m)	self-choice ceremony	*भूमिः (f)	ground / earth

INDECLINABLES

कालेन	in time	*अपि	also / even

ADJECTIVES

*बहु॰	much	विस्मित॰	amazed
अप-हृत॰	carried off	मुक्त॰	freed

DHĀTUS | **VERBS** | **'-त्वा' ENDINGS**

चिन्त्	in thinking	*चिन्तयति	he thinks	चिन्तयित्वा	having thought
पत्	in falling	*पतति	he falls	पतित्वा	having fallen

77

5.5 Story 5

> # BHĪṢMA CARRIES OFF THREE PRINCESSES
>
> Satyavatī's son, Vicitravīrya, becomes king. Bhīṣma, worried that Vicitravīrya is not married, goes to a *svayaṃvara* (see page 71). At the *svayaṃvara*, Bhīṣma carries off three princesses. Bhīṣma grants one of the princesses her freedom, as she is already secretly pledged to someone else, but the other two marry Vicitravīrya.

1. सत्यवत्याः पुत्रः विचित्रवीर्यः नाम।

2. कालेन विचित्रवीर्यः नृपः अभवत्।

3. यदि विचित्रवीर्यस्य भार्या न भविष्यति तर्हि युवराजः न भविष्यति

   इति भीष्मः चिन्तयति स्म।

4. स्वयंवरः आसीत्।

5. बहवः राजपुत्राः स्वयंवरम् अगच्छन्।

[continues on page 80]

Bhīṣma carries off the three princesses.

[continued from page 78]

6. तत् दृष्ट्वा भीष्मः अपि स्वयंवरम् अगच्छत्।

7. स्वयंवरात् भीष्मेण कन्याः अपहृताः।

8. ताः कन्याः अम्बा अम्बिका अम्बालिका च।

9. राजपुत्राः विस्मिताः आसन् भूमिम् अपतन् च।

10. अम्बा भीष्मेण मुक्ता।

11. अम्बिका अम्बालिका च तु विचित्रवीर्यस्य भार्ये अभवताम्॥

From the evidence of this story, what qualities do
you think that Bhīṣma possesses?

5.6 Sanskrit Crossword Puzzle No. 2

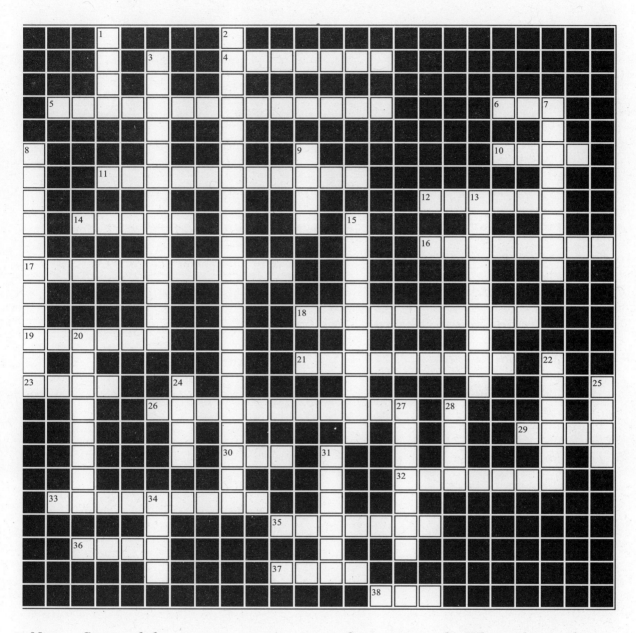

Note: Some of the answers require more than one word. Where this is the case, the numerals shown in brackets (immediately following the clue) refer to the number of letters in each word of the answer.

Across

4. Translate: *anyat.* (7) (see p. 51)

5. Translate: *kutra kanyā asti?* (5, 2, 3, 4)

6. Translate: *idānīm.* (3)

10. Translate: *eṣā.* (4)

11. Translate: *sā śrutā.* (3, 3, 5) (see p.111)

12. Which two prepositions are used in English to translate 3rd case endings? (2, 4)

14. Translate: *agnayaḥ.* (5)

16. Translate the ppp *śruta.* (3, 5)

17. Translate: *nārī dṛṣṭā.* (4, 3, 4)

18. Translate: *naraḥ gataḥ.* (3, 3, 4)

19. Translate: *yadi . . . tarhi . . .* (2, 4)

21. Translate: *vyāpādita* (3, 6)

23. Translate: *acireṇa* (4)

26. Translate: *kim mitram?* (5, 6)

29. Translate: *ṛṣi* (4)

30. What kind of word is *mṛta*? [see p.111] (3)

32. Translate: *kṛta.* (3, 4)

33. Translate: *gurau.* (2, 7)

35. Translate: *dṛṣṭā.* (3, 4)

36. Translate: *etat.* (4)

37. Translate: *mṛta.* (4)

38. Translate: *sarva.* (3)

Down

1. Translate: *agniḥ.* (4)

2. What does 'ppp' mean? (4, 7, 10) (see p. 111)

3. Translate: *tāni khāditāni.* (4, 4, 5) (The first word is 'they')

7. Translate: *kaḥ naraḥ?* (5, 3) (see page 146)

8. Translate: *kāḥ nāryaḥ.* (5, 6) (see p. 147)

9. Translate: *bahu.* (4)

13. Translate: *ukta.* (3, 6)

15. Translate: *dṛṣṭvā.* (6, 4)

20. Translate: *te narāḥ.* (5, 3)

22. Translate: *muninā.* (2, 4)

24. Translate: *kim?* (4)

25. Translate: *kadā?* (4)

27. How were the sons of Śāntanu killed? (7)

28. Translate: *eṣaḥ.* (4)

31. The name of Śāntanu's surviving son. (6) [see p. 41]

34. Translate: *yathā . . . tathā . . .* (2, 2)

CHAPTER SIX

6.1 Epic Civilization: A Day in the Life of a King

In Sanskrit literature, kings are important figures. However, according to the Sanskrit law books, a king cannot just do what he likes; his job demands strict discipline and adherence to duties.

The most important duty for the king is the protection of his subjects and his kingdom. All disciplines are given to support this duty.

He must rise very early in the morning, before sunrise, bathe and perform a sacrifice. Then, he sees his subjects. After that, he takes counsel with his ministers on all sorts of issues, such as alliances, ambassadors, spies and enemies, as well as the needs of his own kingdom. He must fully consider the present and future results of all of his actions, and he must also reflect on what he has done in the past.

He then exercises, bathes and has a meal with his family. Of course, while he eats, he must take precautions against any poisons that his enemies may slip into his food. In the afternoon, he inspects his army. In the evening, he makes another sacrifice to the gods, and then meets with his spies in a secret place. Finally, he has a meal again with his family, listens to music, and then goes to bed at a reasonable hour.

A king listens to the music of a flute.

6.2 The Paradigm of अहम्

अहम् ('I') is called a *personal* pronoun.

The paradigm of अहम् ('I'):

Singular	Dual	Plural
अहम् I	आवाम् we two	वयम् we
माम् me (2nd)	आवाम् us two (2nd)	अस्मान् us (2nd)
मया by me	आवाभ्याम् by us two	अस्माभिः by us
मह्यम् for me	आवाभ्याम् for us two	अस्मभ्यम् for us
मत् from me	आवाभ्याम् from us two	अस्मत् from us
मम of me	आवयोः of us two	अस्माकम् of us
मयि in me	आवयोः in us two	अस्मासु in us

EXERCISE 40

Translate into English or Sanskrit:

1. अहम्
2. अस्माकम्
3. मयि
4. वयम्
5. मम
6. we two
7. we (pl.)
8. me (2nd)
9. by me
10. in us two

EXERCISE 41

In each sentence, choose the correct form from the two in brackets. Next, write out the correct Sanskrit sentence, then translate the sentence into English.

1. अर्जुनः चापम् (मह्यम्, माम्) अददात्।
2. (अस्माभिः, अस्माकम्) गुरुः प्राज्ञः इति शिष्याः अवदन्।
3. राक्षसः (अहम्, माम्) अतुदत्।
4. (अहम्, आवाम्) शान्तनुना सह युद्धम् करोमि।
5. अहो अहो कुत्र (मयि, मम) अश्वः इति नृपः अक्रोशत्।

6.3 Agreement of Verbs with अहम्

A verb can be expressed in one of three Persons. In Sanskrit grammar these are known as:

	Singular	*Dual*	*Plural*
First Person	he/she/it	they two	they
Middle Person	you	you two	you
Best Person	I	we two	we

Later languages (for example, Latin and French) deal with these Persons in the opposite order:

	Singular	*Dual*	*Plural*
First Person	I	we two	we
Second Person	you	you two	you
Third Person	he/she/it	they two	they

In this course, we use the Sanskrit system.

In English, we always use personal pronouns to show the doer of a verb, for example 'I eat', 'you go'. However, in Sanskrit, personal pronouns do not need to be used with verbs. The personal endings on the verbs are all that are needed. You might, however, use a personal pronoun to show emphasis. For example:

अहम् खादामि	=	खादामि	=	'I eat'
वयम् गच्छामः	=	गच्छामः	=	'we go'

EXERCISE 42

Using the table on the preceding page, transliterate the forms below, then give the Person and Number of each, and then translate. For example:

भवसि, *bhavasi,*   Middle Person singular,   'you become'
['Middle Person singular' may be abbreviated to 'Mid. sg.']

1. भवति
2. भवथ
3. भवतः
4. भवन्ति
5. भवावः

6. भवामि
7. भवथः
8. भवसि
9. भवामः

EXERCISE 43

Translate into English, stating the Person and number of each verb:

1. वयम् गृहम् गमिष्यामः ।
2. अहम् हस्तेन वृक्षम् अतुदम् ।
3. अहम् तुभ्यम् फलम् ददामि ।

EXERCISE 44

Translate into Sanskrit, stating the Person and number of each verb:

1. We (pl.) will go to the forest.
2. I speak with my mouth.
3. We (pl.) will see water.
4. I hit the ground with my hand.

6.4   The Sixth Case Ending

The Sixth Case Ending is normally expressed in English by an apostrophe or 'of'. For example:

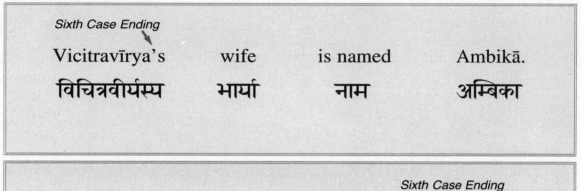

EXERCISE 45

Give two translations for the following Sanskrit phrases. For example:

नरस्य अश्वः

the man's horse / the horse of the man

1. भार्यायाः पुत्राः
2. नराणाम् बुद्धिः
3. सैनिकस्य रथैः
4. तस्य मित्राय
5. नद्याः तीरे

EXERCISE 46

Translate into Sanskrit:

1. The man's dog ran.
2. The dog of the man ran.
3. The Lord's house is large.
4. The elephant eats the fruit of the tree.
5. Bhīṣma's mother is named Gaṅgā.

6.5 Special Use of the Sixth Case Ending

In Sanskrit, the verb 'to have' does not exist. Instead, we use the Sixth Case Ending. For example:

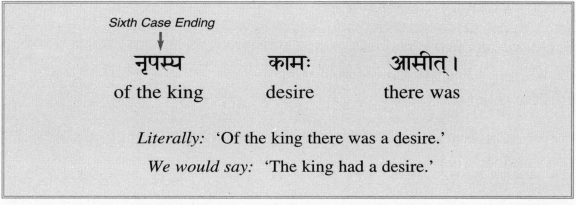

Literally: 'Of the king there was a desire.'

We would say: 'The king had a desire.'

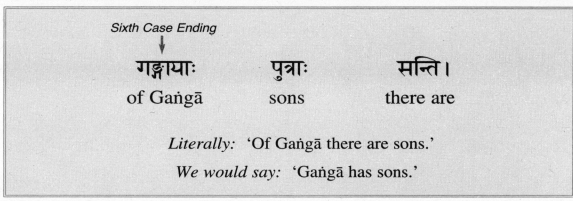

Literally: 'Of Gaṅgā there are sons.'

We would say: 'Gaṅgā has sons.'

EXERCISE 47

Translate into English:

1. नरस्य पुत्रः आसीत् ।
2. पुत्रस्य जनकः अस्ति ।
3. कन्यायाः सोदराः आसन् ।
4. गृहस्य द्वारे न स्तः ।
5. नृपाणाम् राज्यानि सन्ति ।

EXERCISE 48

Translate into Sanskrit:

1. The brave men walk.
2. The bird saw the soldiers.
3. "Go quickly to the house," she said.
4. Once there was a king named Hari.
5. Having eaten, the sage stood.
6. The king had a palace.

Note to teachers: This diagram further develops the family tree shown on page 76.

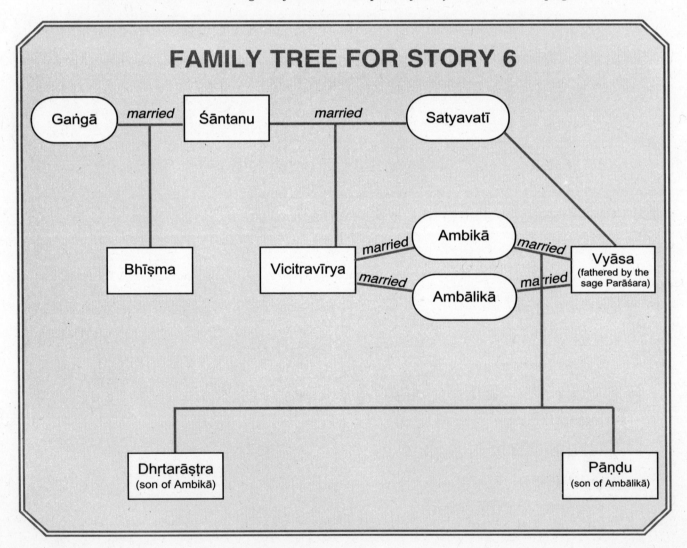

FAMILY TREE FOR STORY 6

Gaṅgā — *married* — Śāntanu — *married* — Satyavatī

Bhīṣma

Vicitravīrya — *married* — Ambikā — *married* — Vyāsa (fathered by the sage Parāśara)

Vicitravīrya — *married* — Ambālikā — *married* — Vyāsa

Dhṛtarāṣṭra (son of Ambikā)

Pāṇḍu (son of Ambālikā)

6.6 Vocabulary for Story 6

*Note to teacher: Words with an asterisk (*) are part of the IGCSE vocabulary.*

NOUNS

व्यासः (m)	Vyāsa	*पतिः (m)	husband
धृतराष्ट्रः (m)	Dhṛtarāṣṭra	*मुखम् (n)	face / mouth
पाण्डुः (m)	Pāṇḍu		

PRONOUNS

*अन्य°   other / another (declines like तत्, सः and सा)

ADJECTIVES

अन्ध°	blind
मुक्त°	freed
पाण्डु°	pale

INDECLINABLE

*तस्मात्   therefore

DHĀTUS

लभ्	in finding
नि + मिष्	in closing the eyes

VERBS

*लभते[1]	he finds
निमिषति	he closes his eyes

‘-त्वा’ ENDINGS

लब्ध्वा	having found
निमिष्य[2]	having closed the eyes

---

[1] Note the वर्धते verb endings (see page 130).

[2] Notice the -य ending instead of -त्वा.

6.7　Story 6

> # WHO WILL BE KING?
>
> Vicitravīrya dies without children. So Bhīṣma arranges for another
> husband, a sage called Vyāsa, to take his place. When Ambikā and
> Ambālikā see the sage, they are shocked. Their negative reactions
> have an effect on their unborn children.

1. विचित्रवीर्यः अचिरेण मृतः अभवत्।

2. भार्ययोः पुत्रः न आसीत्।

3. भीष्मः अचिन्तयत् कथम् अन्यम् नृपम् लप्स्ये इति।

4. सः भार्याभ्याम् अन्यम् पतिम् अलभत।

5. एषः पतिः ऋषिः आसीत्।

6. सः ऋषिः व्यासः नाम।

[continues on page 96]

Ambikā and Ambālikā shocked when they see the sage Vyāsa.

[continued from page 94]

7. ऋषिम् दृष्ट्वा तु अम्बिका निमिषति स्म।

8. तस्मात् तस्याः पुत्रः अन्धः आसीत्।

9. सः पुत्रः धृतराष्ट्रः नाम।

10. यदा अम्बालिका ऋषिम् अपश्यत् तदा तस्याः मुखम्

पाण्डु अभवत्।

11. तस्मात् तस्याः पुत्रः पाण्डुः नाम॥

लप्स्यते *future of* लभते

CHAPTER SEVEN

7.1   Epic Civilization: The Wise

In Sanskrit literature, the help of a sage or wise person often solves a difficult situation. For example, in the last story, Bhīṣma has the difficulty of finding a husband for the two widowed princesses. The sage Vyāsa steps in and offers to marry them.

Being wise means having a deep understanding of the unity of all things: the mind is free from all concern and dwells on the true nature of the One Self.

The wise retain detachment and are able to help with difficult situations because they are free from all ties. Therefore, they can approach problems from a different standpoint and see solutions that ordinary people would not.

7.2 The Paradigms of Nouns Ending in ऋ

In English, the endings **-er** and **-or** on a noun show the agent of an action. For example:

> A swimm**er** swims.
> A sail**or** sails.
> A farm**er** farms.

These endings almost certainly derive from an original ऋ ending which, in Sanskrit, has the same meaning. For example, the masculine word धातृ means 'creator'. Here is its paradigm:

Singular	Dual	Plural
धाता creator	धातारौ two creators	धातारः creators
हे धातः O creator	हे धातारौ O two creators	हे धातारः O creators
धातारम् creator (2nd)	धातारौ two creators (2nd)	धातॄन् creators (2nd)
धात्रा by a creator	धातृभ्याम् by two creators	धातृभिः by creators
धात्रे for a creator	धातृभ्याम् for two creators	धातृभ्यः for creators
धातुः from a creator	धातृभ्याम् from two creators	धातृभ्यः from creators
धातुः of a creator	धात्रोः of two creators	धातॄणाम् of creators
धातरि in a creator	धात्रोः in two creators	धातृषु in creators

Note the 'first-five rule' here. What difference do you notice in the first five case endings? (Remember that the Vocative is also considered as the First case.)

Note also that the word कर्तृ goes like धातृ. It means 'actor' or 'doer'.

98

EXERCISE 49

Decline the word कर्तृ.

EXERCISE 50

A. Translate the following into English:

1. धातारम्
2. कर्तृभ्याम्
3. धातृन्
4. कर्त्रोः
5. कर्तरि
6. धातुः
7. कर्त्रा
8. धातृणाम्
9. धाता
10. कर्ता

B. Translate the following into Sanskrit.

1. from a creator
2. of many actors
3. for an actor
4. by many creators
5. in two creators

7.3 Relationship Nouns

In Sanskrit, many words which describe family relationships end in ऋ. For example:

पितृ (m.)	father	भ्रातृ (m.)	brother
मातृ (f.)	mother	भर्तृ (m.)	husband

The paradigms of पितृ (father) and मातृ (mother) are similar to धातृ *except* for the first two cases. For पितृ the paradigm is as follows:

Singular	Dual	Plural
पिता father	पितरौ two fathers	पितरः fathers
हे पितर् O father	हे पितरौ O two fathers	हे पितरः O fathers
पितरम् father(2nd)	पितरौ two fathers (2nd)	पितॄन् fathers (2nd)
पित्रा by a father	पितृभ्याम् by two fathers	पितृभिः by fathers
पित्रे for a father	पितृभ्याम् for two fathers	पितृभ्यः for fathers
पितुः from a father	पितृभ्याम् from two fathers	पितृभ्यः from fathers
पितुः of a father	पित्रोः of two fathers	पितॄणाम् of fathers
पितरि in a father	पित्रोः in two fathers	पितृषु in fathers

> मातृ goes like पितृ, *except* for the second-case plural मातॄः.
> भर्तृ and भ्रातृ go like पितृ.

100

EXERCISE 51

See if you can recite from memory the paradigms of मातृ and पितृ.

> **BONUS**
> Can you say what is the same and what is different between
> the paradigms of मातृ, पितृ and धातृ ?
> (Hint: the 'First-Five Rule')

EXERCISE 52

Choose the correct form from the two in brackets and write out the correct Sanskrit sentence. Then translate the sentence.

1. (माता, मात्रा) अपठत् ।
2. (धाता, धात्रा) लोकः कृतः ।
3. भार्या (भ्रातुः, भ्रातरम्) प्रत्यवदत् ।
4. (मातुः, माता) नगरम् अगच्छत् ।

EXERCISE 53

Translate the following into English:

1. भर्ता बालकौ अपश्यत् ।
2. सर्वे जनाः धातुः आगच्छन्ति ।
3. पाण्डवाः भ्रातरः ।
4. भर्ता भ्राता च न अवदताम् ।
5. धर्मस्य देवः युधिष्ठिरस्य पिता ।

EXERCISE 54

Choose the correct form from the two in brackets and write out the correct Sanskrit sentence. Then translate the sentence.

1. लोकः (विशालः, विशाला) ।
2. तारका हरिणा (कृतः, कृता) ।
3. (अरुणः, अरुणा) कपिः वृक्षे वसति ।
4. रावणस्य राक्षस्यः (कुपितः, कुपिताः) सन्ति ।
5. (अग्निना, अग्निः) राक्षसौ दग्धौ ।

7.4 The Seventh Case Ending

The Seventh Case Ending is used to show the place where the action happens.
It can be translated as 'in/on', 'at' or 'among'. For example:

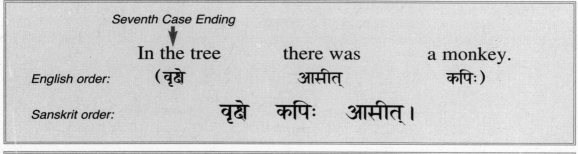

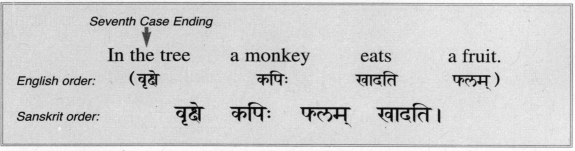

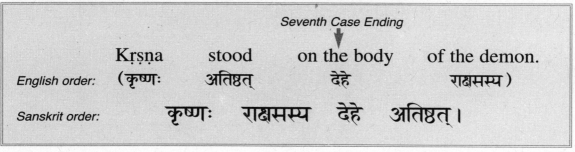

EXERCISE 55

Translate into Sanskrit:

1. The prince lives in the palace.

2. The boy dwelt in the forest.

3. The goddess stands on the mountain.

4. In the sky, there were many birds.

5. At the *svayaṃvara,* the king shoots an arrow.

Note to teachers: This diagram further develops the family tree shown on page 92.

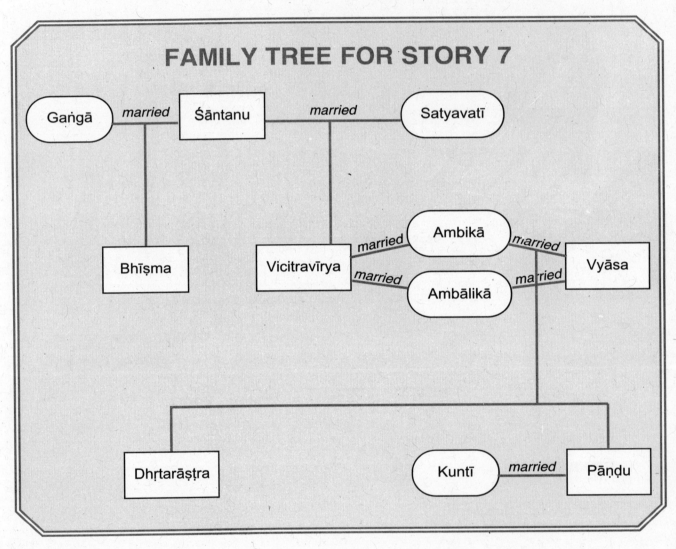

7.5 Vocabulary for Story 7

Note to teacher: Words with an asterisk (*) are part of the IGCSE vocabulary.

NOUNS

*मृगः	(m)	deer	*वनम्	(n)	forest
*शरः	(m)	arrow	कुन्ती	(f)	Kuntī
शापः	(m)	curse	माद्री	(f)	Mādrī

ADJECTIVES

वृत॰	chosen		*द्वितीय॰	second
*तुदित॰	hit			

INDECLINABLES

यस्मात् ... तस्मात्	since ... therefore	*तत्र	there

DHĀTUS · VERBS · '–त्वा' ENDINGS

DHĀTUS		VERBS		'–त्वा' ENDINGS	
कृ	in doing / making	*करोति	he does / makes	कृत्वा	having done / made
अनु+धाव्	in running after	*अनुधावति	he runs after	अनुधाव्य[1]	having run after

[1] *Notice the य ending instead of त्वा.*

7.6　Story 7

A DEER CURSES PĀṆḌU

Pāṇḍu becomes king, and Kuntī chooses him as a husband. While hunting, Pāṇḍu accidentally kills a sage who is disguised as a deer. The sage curses Pāṇḍu, saying that when he embraces his wife, he will die.

1. यस्मात् धृतराष्ट्रः अन्धः तस्मात् पाण्डुः नृपः अभवत्।

2. पाण्डुः अचिन्तयत् का मम भार्या भविष्यति इति।

3. सः कुन्त्याः स्वयंवरम् अगच्छत्।

4. पाण्डुः कुन्त्या वृतः।

5. भीष्मः पाण्डवे द्वितीयाम् भार्याम् अलभत।

6. सा माद्री नाम।

7. विवाहम् कृत्वा पाण्डुः भार्याभ्याम् सह वनम् अगच्छत्।

[continues on page 108]

A sage, disguised as a dying deer, curses Pāṇḍu.

[continued from page 106]

8. तत्र पाण्डुः मृगम् अनुधावति स्म।

9. शरेण तुदितः मृगः शापम् अवदत् यदि त्वम् भार्याम् परिष्वजसे

तर्हि मृतः भविष्यसि इति॥

परिष्वजसे 'you embrace' (परि + स्वज्)

CHAPTER EIGHT

8.1   Epic Civilization: Mantras

Mantras are special words having special powers. Some mantras can summon gods, like the mantra Kuntī uses in the next story. Others can lead to attainment of a particular goal, such as the gaining of a power, or union with God.

Mantras can be single syllables, a word, or a group of words. The correct pronunciation of a mantra is very important. If wrongly pronounced, it can have the wrong effect. Mantras are often repeated. They are most powerful when repeated mentally rather than aloud.

A girl being given a mantra.

8.2 The Passive Sentence

There are two ways to say a sentence. One is in an active way, such as:

The boy <u>kicks</u> the football.

Another is in a passive way, such as:

The football <u>is kicked</u> by the boy.

What do you notice about the verbs used in both sentences?

EXERCISE 56

Here are some English sentences. Say whether they are active or passive.

1. The warrior <u>**hits**</u> the demon.
2. The demon <u>**is hit**</u> by the warrior.
3. Bhīṣma <u>**goes**</u> to do battle.
4. A song <u>**is sung**</u> by the lady.
5. The play <u>**was performed**</u> by the actors.

EXERCISE 57

Here are some active sentences. Rewrite them in the passive.

1. The soldier kills the dragon.
2. The lady finds the man.
3. Bhīṣma sees the snake.
4. The queen walks to the palace.
5. The boy throws a ball.

8.3 The Past Passive Sentence in Sanskrit

Past passive sentences in Sanskrit often use -त ending words such as हत, दृष्ट and श्रुत. These words are called 'past passive participles' (ppp). Note that 'was/were' or 'has/have been' usually is assumed but not stated in Sanskrit. Here are some examples:

-त *Ending Word*

राक्षसः   नरेण   हतः ।

demon   by man   killed

The demon was killed by the man.

-त *Ending Word*

वृक्षाः   अर्जुनेन   दृष्टाः ।

trees   by Arjuna   seen

The trees were seen by Arjuna.

-त *Ending Word*

शब्दः   नार्या   श्रुतः ।

sound   by lady   heard

The sound has been heard by the lady.

EXERCISE 58

Translate the following sentences into English. Some are active and some are passive.

1. बालकः गुरून् अगच्छत्।
2. गुरुः बालकान् अगच्छत्।
3. गुरुः बालकेन श्रुतः।
4. गुरवः बालकेन श्रुताः।
5. नौका कन्यया दृष्टा।

8.4 Revision of the Conjugation of वर्धते

There are some verbs that take a different set of endings to भवति. As an example, we shall use वर्धते, meaning 'grows'.

The paradigm of the **Present Tense** of वर्धते is:

Singular	*Dual*	*Plural*
वर्धते he, she, it grows	वर्धेते they two grow	वर्धन्ते they grow
वर्धसे you grow	वर्धेथे you two grow	वर्धध्वे you grow
वर्धे I grow	वर्धावहे we two grow	वर्धामहे we grow

Note: The endings of वर्धते are translated in exactly the same way as भवति.

EXERCISE 59

Conjugate the following stems in the Present Tense, using the वर्धते endings:

(a) लभते (finds)   (b) स्वजते (embraces)

112

8.5 Past and Present Passive Verbs

We have already learned the way in which a *past* passive sentence can be constructed using a -त ending word. For example:

अर्जुनः कुन्त्या दृष्टः ।   Arjuna was seen by Kuntī.

Another way to form a passive sentence is by using a *present* passive verb. This is formed simply by adding the ending -य directly on to the root. The वर्धते endings are then added instead of those for भवति. For example:

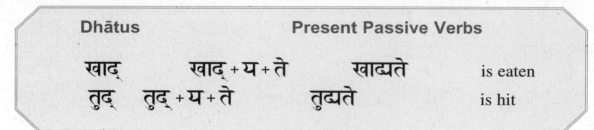

Dhātus		Present Passive Verbs	
खाद्	खाद् + य + ते	खाद्यते	is eaten
तुद्	तुद् + य + ते	तुद्यते	is hit

Here are some sentences using these present passive verbal forms:

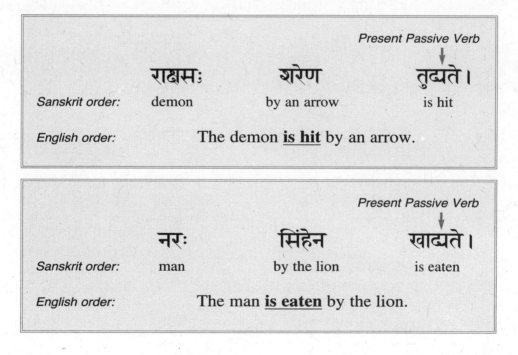

			Present Passive Verb ↓
	राक्षसः	शरेण	तुद्यते ।
Sanskrit order:	demon	by an arrow	is hit
English order:	The demon **is hit** by an arrow.		

			Present Passive Verb ↓
	नरः	सिंहेन	खाद्यते ।
Sanskrit order:	man	by the lion	is eaten
English order:	The man **is eaten** by the lion.		

113

Here is a list of several *dhātus* with their present active and passive verb forms. Some are irregular.

DHĀTUS	PRESENT ACTIVE		PRESENT PASSIVE	
दा	*ददाति	gives	दीयते	he/she/it is given
पा	*पिबति	drinks	पीयते	he/she/it is drunk
तुद्	*तुदति	hits	तुद्यते	he/she/it is hit
खाद्	*खादति	eats	खाद्यते	he/she/it is eaten
पठ्	*पठति	reads	पठ्यते	he/she/it is read
श्रु	श्रृणोति	hears	श्रूयते	he/she/it is heard
कृ	*करोति	makes/does	क्रियते	he/she/it is made/done
चिन्त्	*चिन्तयति	thinks	चिन्त्यते	he/she/it is thought
गम्	*गच्छति	goes	गम्यते	he/she/it is gone to
लभ्	*लभते	finds	लभ्यते	he/she/it is found
वद्	*वदति	speaks	उद्यते	he/she/it is spoken
कथ्	कथयति	tells	कथ्यते	he/she/it is told
दृश्	*पश्यति	sees	दृश्यते	he/she/it is seen

RULES FOR PRESENT PASSIVE VERBS

1. The object ('the done to') is expressed in the First Case and the subject is in the Third Case.

2. The verb (the action) has a य after the dhātu.

3. The ending of the verb takes a वर्धते form.

4. The ending of the verb agrees in number with the word in the First Case, i.e., with the object of the action.

Here is an example of the paradigm of the **Present Passive:**

Singular	*Dual*	*Plural*
खाद्यते	खाद्येते	खाद्यन्ते
he, she, it is eaten	they two are eaten	they are eaten
खाद्यसे	खाद्येथे	खाद्यध्वे
you are eaten	you two are eaten	you are eaten
खाद्ये	खाद्यावहे	खाद्यामहे
I am eaten	we two are eaten	we are eaten

EXERCISE 60

Translate into English. Pay close attention to whether the verb is active or passive.

1. पीयते
2. चिन्त्यते
3. दृश्येते
4. श्रूयन्ते
5. पठ्यते

6. खादति
7. चिन्तयति
8. कथ्यते
9. लभते
10. उद्यन्ते

A river is found by a lion.

8.6 Further Rules of Translation

In addition to the Golden Rules of Translation on page 21, there are the following:

A For sentences with more than one action, the different actions should be tackled one by one in the order they appear in the sentence, each with their doer and object before it. This will include -त्वा words.

B Often, the doer will not be separately mentioned, but is understood from the ending of the verb.

C When the verb is a form of अस्ति ('is'), it is often left out. For example: रामः वीरः। ('Rāma is brave.')

D With forms of भवति/अस्ति there is no object. For example: रामः नृपः भवति। ('Rāma becomes king.')

E When there is an इति in a sentence, indicating the end of a statement or thought, there may be an extra verb in the sentence, the one which is part of what is said or thought. For example: सिंहम् पश्यामि इति सः अवदत्। ("I see the lion", he said.)

F If a verb is in the past tense, it will usually begin with an अ and have past tense endings. You will often find this form in the vocabulary without the अ and in its present form, unless it is a special case.

EXERCISE 61

Translate into English:

1. शरम् कृत्वा नरः वनम् अगच्छत्।
2. मृगम् अनुधावति।
3. सीता गता।
4. कुक्कुरः सिंहः भवति।
5. मृगम् पश्यामि इति सा अवदत्।

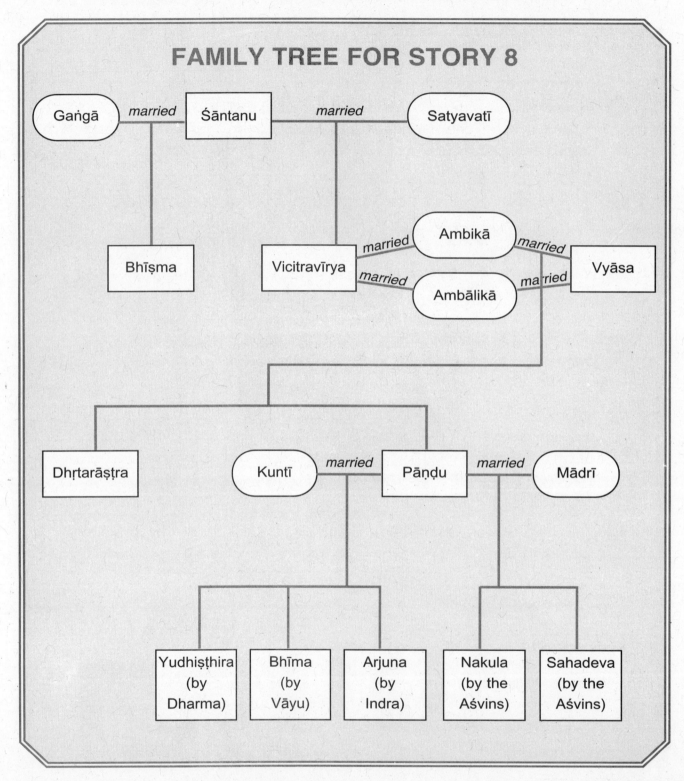

FAMILY TREE FOR STORY 8

8.7 Vocabulary for Story 8

Note to teacher: Words with an asterisk (*) are part of the IGCSE vocabulary.

NOUNS

मन्त्रः (m)	mantra		युधिष्ठिरः (m)	Yudhiṣṭhira
*देवः (m)	god		भीमः (m)	Bhīma
*सूर्यः (m)	sun		अर्जुनः (m)	Arjuna
*कर्णः (m)	Karṇa		नकुलः (m)	Nakula
*वचनम् (n)	word		सहदेवः (m)	Sahadeva

ADJECTIVES

त्यक्त॰	abandoned		*पञ्च॰	five
*जात॰	born			

DHĀTU   VERB   '-त्वा' ENDING

DHĀTU		VERB		'-त्वा' ENDING	
दा	in giving	*ददाति	he gives	दत्त्वा	having given

119

8.8 Story 8

THE PĀṆḌAVAS ARE BORN

Because of the deer's curse, Pāṇḍu cannot have children. However, when Kuntī was a teenager, she had been given a magical word (mantra) to give birth to three sons. Yudhiṣṭhira is fathered by Dharma, the god of law. Bhīma is fathered by Vāyu, the god of the wind. Arjuna is fathered by Indra, the king of the gods. Kuntī also shares the magical word with Mādrī, who gives birth to the twins Nakula and Sahadeva, who are fathered by the Aśvins, the twin gods of the dawn.

1. मृगस्य वचनानि श्रुत्वा पाण्डुः दुःखेन अचिन्तयत् कथम्

   मम पुत्राः भविष्यन्ति इति।

2. पुरा तु यदा कुन्ती कन्या तदा ऋषिः तस्यै कम् अपि मन्त्रम् अददात्।

3. तेन मन्त्रेण कः चन देवः तुभ्यम् पुत्रम् दास्यति इति ऋषिः अवदत्।

4. सूर्यम् चिन्तयित्वा कुन्ती मन्त्रम् अवदत्।

5. सूर्यः ताम् आगम्य तस्यै पुत्रम् अददात्।

[continues on page 122]

The Pāṇḍavas

121

[continued from page 120]

6. सः पुत्रः कर्णः नाम।

7. कर्णः तु कुन्त्या त्यक्तः।

8. एवम् पञ्च पुत्राः मन्त्रेण जाताः।

9. तेषाम् जनकाः देवाः।

10. ते युधिष्ठिरः भीमः अर्जुनः नकुलः सहदेवः च॥

दास्यति 'will give'

8.9 Sanskrit Crossword Puzzle No. 3

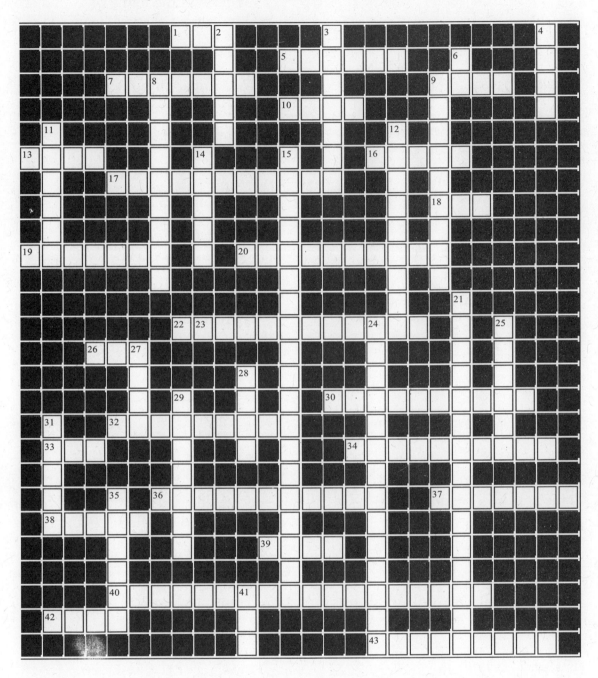

Note: Some of the answers require more than one word. Where this is the case, the numerals shown in brackets (immediately following the clue) refer to the number of letters in each word of the answer.

Across

1. *Vṛta* means 'chosen'. What kind of word is it? (3)

5. Translate: *bhūmi*. (6)

7. Translate: *patiḥ*. (7)

9. Translate the pronoun *mayā*. (2, 2)

10. Translate: *kadā?* (4)

13. Translate: *tīram*. (4)

16. Translate: *kutra?* (5)

17. Translate: *kasmin nagare*. (2, 5, 4)

18. *Sarva* is a pronoun declined like *saḥ, sā* and *tat*. Translate. (3)

19. Translate: *dhātā*. (7)

20. Translate: *naraḥ api*. (3, 3, 4)

22. Ambikā and Ambālikā were the wives of which king? (12)

26. Translate: *kaḥ?* (3)

30. Translate: *kim vanam*. (4, 6)

32. Translate: *kena cit*. (2, 7) (see p.73)

33. Translate: *tvam*. (3)

34. What are the three words used for an indefinite expression? (3, 4, 3)

36. What was the name of Ambikā's first son? (11)

37. Translate: *saḥ labhate*. (2, 5)

[continued next page]

Down

2. What was the name of Ambālikā's first son? (5)

3. Translate: *Kaḥ cit naraḥ*. (4, 3)

4. Which paradigm does the word *vāyu* decline like?

6. Translate: *mama*. (2)

8. Translate: *kutra cit*. (9)

9. Translate: *dhātrā*. (2, 7)

11. Translate: *janaka*. (6)

12. Translate: *kā nārī*. (5, 4)

14. Sanskrit has no verb for 'has / have'. Which case is used to express it? (5)

15. Translate: *mātṛ, bhrātṛ, pitṛ*. (6, 7, 6)

21. Translate: *rājaputraḥ cintayati*. (3, 6, 6)

23. Translate: *aham*. (1)

24. Which three paradigms (masculine, feminine and neuter) are used for adjectives ending in '*a*'? (4, 4, 6)

25. The name of Śāntanu's eighth son. (6)

27. Translate: *eva*. (4)

28. Give two English prepositions used to translate the seventh case. (2, 2)

29. Translate: *katham api*. (7)

31. The second husband of Ambikā and Ambālikā was a great sage. What was his name? (5)

[continued next page]

38. A *śara* is used with a bow. (5)

39. Translate: *kim*. (4)

40. Translate: *pitaraḥ gatāḥ*. (3,7,4,4)
    (Hint: 1st word is 'the', 3rd word is 'were'.)

42. *bahu* is a pronoun declined like *saḥ, sā* or *tat*. Translate. (4)

43. *karoti* has two meanings. What are they? (5,4)

35. With which case is the verb *dadāti* 'to give' used? (6)

41. Translate: *katham*. (3)

APPENDICES

APPENDIX 1

Transliteration

The word 'transliteration' here means the writing of Sanskrit using English letters. This Appendix shows all the Sanskrit devanāgarī letters together with the English letters used to represent them.

1. VOWELS

अ	आ	इ	ई	उ	ऊ	ऋ	ॠ	ए	ऐ	ओ	औ
a	ā	i	ī	u	ū	ṛ	ṝ	e	ai	o	au
क	का	कि	की	कु	कू	कृ	कॄ	के	कै	को	कौ
ka	kā	ki	kī	ku	kū	kṛ	kṝ	ke	kai	ko	kau

2. CONSONANTS

क	ka	च	ca	ट	ṭa	त	ta	प	pa
ख	kha	छ	cha	ठ	ṭha	थ	tha	फ	pha
ग	ga	ज	ja	ड	ḍa	द	da	ब	ba
घ	gha	झ	jha	ढ	ḍha	ध	dha	भ	bha
ङ	ṅa	ञ	ña	ण	ṇa	न	na	म	ma
ह	ha	य	ya	र	ra	ल	la	व	va
		श	śa	ष	ṣa	स	sa		

:	ḥ	ं	ṃ

3. HALANTA CONSONANTS

For halanta letters, the 'a' of the letter is dropped. Examples:

क् k	म् m	ट् ṭ	घ् gh	श् ś

4. JOINED CONSONANTS

(a) Standard Examples

स्य sya	ग्न gna	न्त nta	ल्प lpa	ष्प ṣpa

(b) Double-decker Examples

क्क kka	द्व dva	ङ्ग ṅga

(c) Examples of Consonants Joined with र

त्र tra	प्र pra	क्र kra	ग्र gra	ब्र bra
र्त rta	र्प rpa	र्क rka	र्ग rga	र्ब rba

(d) Some Exceptional Joined Consonants

क्ष kṣa	श्र śra	ज्ञ jña	क्त kta	ह्र hra

APPENDIX 2

Paradigms

A paradigm is an example of all the forms and endings of a word set out as a list or chart, and which is often used as a pattern for other words of a similar kind. All the paradigms used in this volume, as well as those of the earlier Sanskrit textbooks in this series, are included in this Appendix for easy reference.

VERBS

भवति — Present Tense:

Singular	Dual	Plural
भवति he, she, it becomes	भवतः they two become	भवन्ति they become
भवसि you become	भवथः you two become	भवथ you become
भवामि I become	भवावः we two become	भवामः we become

भवति — Future Tense:

Singular	Dual	Plural
भविष्यति he, she, it will become	भविष्यतः they two will become	भविष्यन्ति they will become
भविष्यसि you will become	भविष्यथः you two will become	भविष्यथ you will become
भविष्यामि I shall become	भविष्यावः we two shall become	भविष्यामः we shall become

भवति — Past Tense:

Singular	Dual	Plural
अभवत् he, she, it became	अभवताम् they two became	अभवन् they became
अभवः you became	अभवतम् you two became	अभवत you became
अभवम् I became	अभवाव we two became	अभवाम we became

वर्धते — Present Tense:

Singular	Dual	Plural
वर्धते he, she, it grows	वर्धेते they two grow	वर्धन्ते they grow
वर्धसे you grow	वर्धेथे you two grow	वर्धध्वे you grow
वर्धे I grow	वर्धावहे we two grow	वर्धामहे we grow

वर्धते — Future Tense:

Singular	Dual	Plural
वर्धिष्यते he, she, it will grow	वर्धिष्येते they two will grow	वर्धिष्यन्ते they will grow
वर्धिष्यसे you will grow	वर्धिष्येथे you two will grow	वर्धिष्यध्वे you will grow
वर्धिष्ये I shall grow	वर्धिष्यावहे we two shall grow	वर्धिष्यामहे we shall grow

वर्धते — Past Tense:

Singular	Dual	Plural
अवर्धत he, she, it grew	अवर्धेताम् they two grew	अवर्धन्त they grew
अवर्धथाः you grew	अवर्धेथाम् you two grew	अवर्धध्वम् you grew
अवर्धे I grew	अवर्धावहि we two grew	अवर्धामहि we grew

लभते — Future Tense:

Singular	Dual	Plural
लप्स्यते he, she, it will find	लप्स्येते they two will find	लप्स्यन्ते they will find
लप्स्यसे you will find	लप्स्येथे you two will find	लप्स्यध्वे you will find
लप्स्ये I shall find	लप्स्यावहे we two shall find	लप्स्यामहे we shall find

खादति — Present Tense Passive:

Singular	Dual	Plural
खाद्यते he, she, it is eaten	खाद्येते they two are eaten	खाद्यन्ते they are eaten
खाद्यसे you are eaten	खाद्येथे you two are eaten	खाद्यध्वे you are eaten
खाद्ये I am eaten	खाद्यावहे we two are eaten	खाद्यामहे we are eaten

अस्ति — Present Tense:

Singular	Dual	Plural
अस्ति he, she, it is	स्तः they two are	सन्ति they are
असि you are	स्थः you two are	स्थ you are
अस्मि I am	स्वः we two are	स्मः we are

अस्ति — Past Tense:

Singular	Dual	Plural
आसीत् he, she, it was	आस्ताम् they two were	आसन् they were
आसीः you were	आस्तम् you two were	आस्त you were
आसम् I was	आस्व we two were	आस्म we were

For nouns, see next page.

NOUNS

रामः (Rāma): paradigm for masculine nouns ending in अ

Singular	Dual	Plural
रामः Rāma	रामौ two Rāmas	रामाः Rāmas
हे राम O Rāma	हे रामौ O two Rāmas	हे रामाः O Rāmas
रामम् Rāma (2nd)	रामौ two Rāmas (2nd)	रामान् Rāmas (2nd)
रामेण by Rāma	रामाभ्याम् by two Rāmas	रामैः by Rāmas
रामाय for Rāma	रामाभ्याम् for two Rāmas	रामेभ्यः for Rāmas
रामात् from Rāma	रामाभ्याम् from two Rāmas	रामेभ्यः from Rāmas
रामस्य of Rāma	रामयोः of two Rāmas	रामाणाम् of Rāmas
रामे in Rāma	रामयोः in two Rāmas	रामेषु in Rāmas

मित्रम् ('friend'): paradigm for neuter nouns ending in अम्

Singular	Dual	Plural
मित्रम् friend	मित्रे two friends	मित्राणि friends
हे मित्र O friend	हे मित्रे O two friends	हे मित्राणि O friends
मित्रम् friend (2nd)	मित्रे two friends (2nd)	मित्राणि friends (2nd)
मित्रेण by a friend	मित्राभ्याम् by two friends	मित्रैः by friends
मित्राय for a friend	मित्राभ्याम् for two friends	मित्रेभ्यः for friends
मित्रात् from a friend	मित्राभ्याम् from two friends	मित्रेभ्यः from friends
मित्रस्य of a friend	मित्रयोः of two friends	मित्राणाम् of friends
मित्रे in a friend	मित्रयोः in two friends	मित्रेषु in friends

सीता (Sītā): paradigm for feminine nouns ending in आ

Singular	Dual	Plural
सीता Sītā	सीते two Sītās	सीताः Sītās
हे सीते O Sītā	हे सीते O two Sītās	हे सीताः O Sītās
सीताम् Sītā (2nd)	सीते two Sītās (2nd)	सीताः Sītās (2nd)
सीतया by Sītā	सीताभ्याम् by two Sītās	सीताभिः by Sītās
सीतायै for Sītā	सीताभ्याम् for two Sītās	सीताभ्यः for Sītās
सीतायाः from Sītā	सीताभ्याम् from two Sītās	सीताभ्यः from Sītās
सीतायाः of Sītā	सीतयोः of two Sītās	सीतानाम् of Sītās
सीतायाम् in Sītā	सीतयोः in two Sītās	सीतासु in Sītās

नदी ('river'): paradigm for feminine nouns ending in ई

Singular	Dual	Plural
नदी river	नद्यौ two rivers	नद्यः rivers
हे नदि O river	हे नद्यौ O two rivers	हे नद्यः O rivers
नदीम् river (2nd)	नद्यौ two rivers (2nd)	नदीः rivers (2nd)
नद्या by a river	नदीभ्याम् by two rivers	नदीभिः by rivers
नद्यै for a river	नदीभ्याम् for two rivers	नदीभ्यः for rivers
नद्याः from a river	नदीभ्याम् from two rivers	नदीभ्यः from rivers
नद्याः of a river	नद्योः of two rivers	नदीनाम् of rivers
नद्याम् in a river	नद्योः in two rivers	नदीषु in rivers

136

हरिः ('Lord'): paradigm for masculine nouns ending in इ

Singular	Dual	Plural
हरिः Lord	हरी two Lords	हरयः Lords
हे हरे O Lord	हे हरी O two Lords	हे हरयः O Lords
हरिम् Lord (2nd)	हरी two Lords (2nd)	हरीन् Lords (2nd)
हरिणा by the Lord	हरिभ्याम् by two Lords	हरिभिः by Lords
हरये for the Lord	हरिभ्याम् for two Lords	हरिभ्यः for Lords
हरेः from the Lord	हरिभ्याम् from two Lords	हरिभ्यः from Lords
हरेः of the Lord	हर्योः of two Lords	हरीणाम् of Lords
हरौ in the Lord	हर्योः in two Lords	हरिषु in Lords

137

गुरुः ('teacher'): paradigm for masculine nouns ending in -उ

Singular	Dual	Plural
गुरुः teacher	गुरू two teachers	गुरवः teachers
हे गुरो O teacher	हे गुरू O two teachers	हे गुरवः O teachers
गुरुम् teacher (2nd)	गुरू two teachers (2nd)	गुरुन् teachers (2nd)
गुरुणा by the teacher	गुरुभ्याम् by two teachers	गुरुभिः by teachers
गुरवे for the teacher	गुरुभ्याम् for two teachers	गुरुभ्यः for teachers
गुरोः from the teacher	गुरुभ्याम् from two teachers	गुरुभ्यः from teachers
गुरोः of the teacher	गुर्वोः of two teachers	गुरुणाम् of teachers
गुरौ in the teacher	गुर्वोः in two teachers	गुरुषु in teachers

धातृ ('creator'): paradigm for masculine agent nouns ending in -ऋ

Singular	Dual	Plural
धाता creator	धातारौ two creators	धातारः creators
हे धातः O creator	हे धातारौ O two creators	हे धातारः O creators
धातारम् creator	धातारौ two creators (2nd)	धातॄन् creators
धात्रा by a creator	धातृभ्याम् by two creators	धातृभिः by creators
धात्रे for a creator	धातृभ्याम् for two creators	धातृभ्यः for creators
धातुः from a creator	धातृभ्याम् from two creators	धातृभ्यः from creators
धातुः of a creator	धात्रोः of two creators	धातॄणाम् of creators
धातरि in a creator	धात्रोः in two creators	धातृषु in creators

पितृ ('father'): paradigm for many masculine relationship nouns ending in –ऋ

Singular	Dual	Plural
पिता father	पितरौ two fathers	पितरः fathers
हे पितर् O father	हे पितरौ O two fathers	हे पितरः O fathers
पितरम् father	पितरौ two fathers (2nd)	पितॄन् fathers
पित्रा by a father	पितृभ्याम् by two fathers	पितृभिः by fathers
पित्रे for a father	पितृभ्याम् for two fathers	पितृभ्यः for fathers
पितुः from a father	पितृभ्याम् from two fathers	पितृभ्यः from fathers
पितुः of a father	पित्रोः of two fathers	पितॄणाम् of fathers
पितरि in a father	पित्रोः in two fathers	पितृषु in fathers

140

मातृ ('mother'): paradigm for many feminine relationship nouns ending in –ऋ

Singular	Dual	Plural
माता mother	मातरौ two mothers	मातरः mothers
हे मातर् O mother	हे मातरौ O two mothers	हे मातरः O mothers
मातरम् mother	मातरौ two mothers (2nd)	मातॄः mothers
मात्रा by a mother	मातृभ्याम् by two mothers	मातृभिः by mothers
मात्रे for a mother	मातृभ्याम् for two mothers	मातृभ्यः for mothers
मातुः from a mother	मातृभ्याम् from two mothers	मातृभ्यः from mothers
मातुः of a mother	मात्रोः of two mothers	मातॄणाम् of mothers
मातरि in a mother	मात्रोः in two mothers	मातृषु in mothers

For pronouns, see next page.

PRONOUNS

The *neuter* paradigm for the pronoun तत् ('that'):

Singular	Dual	Plural
तत् that	ते those two	तानि those
तत् that (2nd)	ते those two (2nd)	तानि those (2nd)
तेन by that	ताभ्याम् by those two	तैः by those
तस्मै for that	ताभ्याम् for those two	तेभ्यः for those
तस्मात् from that	ताभ्याम् from those two	तेभ्यः from those
तस्य of that	तयोः of those two	तेषाम् of those
तस्मिन् in that	तयोः in those two	तेषु in those

Note: In the dual and plural, 2nd Ending onwards,
sometimes तत् is translated as 'them'.

142

The *masculine* paradigm for the pronoun तत् ('he / that'):

Singular	Dual	Plural
सः he, that	तौ those two	ते those
तम् him, that (2nd)	तौ those two (2nd)	तान् those (2nd)
तेन by him, by that	ताभ्याम् by those two	तैः by those
तस्मै for him, for that	ताभ्याम् for those two	तेभ्यः for those
तस्मात् from him, from that	ताभ्याम् from those two	तेभ्यः from those
तस्य of him, of that	तयोः of those two	तेषाम् of those
तस्मिन् in him, in that	तयोः in those two	तेषु in those

*Note: In the dual and plural, 2nd Ending onwards,
sometimes तत् is translated as 'them'.*

143

The _feminine_ paradigm for the pronoun तत् ('she / that'):

Singular	Dual	Plural
सा she, that	ते those two	ताः those
ताम् her, that (2nd)	ते those two (2nd)	ताः those (2nd)
तया by her, by that	ताभ्याम् by those two	ताभिः by those
तस्यै for her, for that	ताभ्याम् for those two	ताभ्यः for those
तस्याः from her, from that	ताभ्याम् from those two	ताभ्यः from those
तस्याः of her, of that	तयोः of those two	तासाम् of those
तस्याम् in her, in that	तयोः in those two	तासु in those

Note: In the dual and plural, 2nd Ending onwards,
sometimes तत् _is translated as 'them'._

144

The paradigm of the *neuter* question word किम् ('what? / which?'):

Singular	Dual	Plural
किम् what? / which?	के which two?	कानि which?
किम् to what? / to which? (2nd)	के to which two? (2nd)	कानि to which? (2nd)
केन by what? / by which?	काभ्याम् by which two?	कैः by which?
कस्मै for what? / for which?	काभ्याम् for which two?	केभ्यः for which?
कस्मात् from what?/from which?	काभ्याम् from which two?	केभ्यः from which?
कस्य of what? / of which?	कयोः of which two?	केषाम् of which?
कस्मिन् in what? / in which?	कयोः in which two?	केषु in which?

145

The paradigm of the *masculine* question word कः ('who? / which?'):

Singular	Dual	Plural
कः who? / which?	कौ which two?	के which?
कम् to whom? / to which?	कौ to which two? (2nd)	कान् to which?
केन by whom? / by which?	काभ्याम् by which two?	कैः by which?
कस्मै for whom? / for which?	काभ्याम् for which two?	केभ्यः for which?
कस्मात् from whom?/ from which?	काभ्याम् from which two?	केभ्यः from which?
कस्य of whom?/ of which?	कयोः of which two?	केषाम् of which?
कस्मिन् in whom? / in which?	कयोः in which two?	केषु in which?

The paradigm of the *feminine* question word का ('who? / which?'):

Singular	Dual	Plural
का who? / which?	के which two?	काः which?
काम् to whom? / to which?	के to which two? (2nd)	काः to which? (2nd)
कया by whom? / by which?	काभ्याम् by which two?	काभिः by which?
कस्यै for whom? / for which?	काभ्याम् for which two?	काभ्यः for which?
कस्याः from whom? / from which?	काभ्याम् from which two?	काभ्यः from which?
कस्याः of whom? / of which?	कयोः of which two?	कासाम् of which?
कस्याम् in whom? / in which?	कयोः in which two?	कासु in which?

147

The paradigm of अहम् ('I'):

Singular	Dual	Plural
अहम् I	आवाम् we two	वयम् we
माम् me (2nd)	आवाम् us two (2nd)	अस्मान् us (2nd)
मया by me	आवाभ्याम् by us two	अस्माभिः by us
मह्यम् for me	आवाभ्याम् for us two	अस्मभ्यम् for us
मत् from me	आवाभ्याम् from us two	अस्मत् from us
मम of me	आवयोः of us two	अस्माकम् of us
मयि in me	आवयोः in us two	अस्मासु in us

APPENDIX 3

Vocabulary: English – Sanskrit

This English–Sanskrit vocabulary comprises in alphabetical order the appropriate English renderings of all the Sanskrit words used in the exercises and stories found in this volume, as well as those used in the earlier Sanskrit textbooks, 'The Stories of Krishna' and 'The Story of Rāma'.

A

abandoned	त्यक्त॰
actor, doer	कर्तृ (m.)
afraid	भीत॰
again	पुनः
again and again	पुनः पुनः
Agha, name of a demon	अघः
alas! alas!	हा हा
(sets) alight	दाह्यति
all	सर्व॰
alone, only	एव (emphasises previous word)
also, even	अपि
amazed	विस्मित॰
Ambālikā	अम्बालिका
Ambā	अम्बा
Ambikā	अम्बिका
and	च
angry	कुपित॰

another	अन्य॰
answers, replies	प्रतिवदति
are – they (plural) are	सन्ति
– they two are	स्तः
– we (plural) are	स्मः
– we two are	स्वः
– you (sing.) are	असि
– you (plural) are	स्थ
– you two are	स्थः
Arjuna	अर्जुनः
army	सेना
arrow	शरः
as if, like	इव
ask	पृच्छ
asked	अपृच्छत्
(having) asked	पृष्ट्वा
asks	पृच्छति
asks for	प्रार्थयति
Aśoka trees	अशोक-वृक्षाः
ate	अखादत्
Ayodhyā	अयोध्या

B

bank (of a river)	तीरम्
battle	युद्धम्
(makes) battle	युद्धम् करोति
beast	पशु (m.)
beautiful	रमणीय॰, रुचिर॰
became	अभवत्
be!, become!	भव (sg.),
	भवत (pl.)
(having) become	भूत्वा
(will) become	भविष्यति
becomes	भवति
belly	उदरः
best	उत्तम॰
Bharata	भरतः
Bhīma	भीमः
Bhīṣma	भीष्मः
binds	बध्नाति
bird	खगः
black	कृष्ण॰
blind	अन्ध॰
bliss	आनन्दः
blood	रक्तम्
blue	नील॰
boat	नौका
body	देहः
book	पुस्तकम्
born	जात॰

(having) bound	बद्ध्वा
bow [the noun]	चापः
bowed	अनमत्
(having) bowed	नत्वा
bows [the verb]	नमति
boy	बालकः
Brahmā weapon	ब्रह्मास्त्रम्
brave	वीर॰
breakfast	प्रातराशः
breast	स्तनः
bring!	आनय
brings	आनयति
brother	सोदरः, भ्रातृ (m.)
brought	आनयत्
built	अकरोत्
(will) burn	धक्ष्यति
burned	अदहत्
burns	दहति
burnt	दग्ध॰
(having) burnt	दग्ध्वा
but	तु
butter	नवनीतम्

C

calf	वत्सः
came	आगच्छत्

Cāṇūra	चाणूरः
carried off	अपहृत॰
causeway	सेतुः
cave	गुहा
(a) certain	एक॰
chair	पीठम्
chariot	रथः
cheating; sin	अधर्मः
chin	चिबुकम्
chosen	वृत॰
city, town	नगरम्
climbs	आरोहति
closes (the eyes)	निमिषति
(having) closed the eyes	निमिष्य
cloud	मेघः
colour	वर्णः
come	आगत॰
(having) come	आगम्य
(will) come	आगमिष्यति
comes	आगच्छति
come!	आगच्छ
conquered	जित॰, अजयत्
conquers, is victorious	जयति
contented	संतुष्ट॰
cowherd	गोपालः
Creator, the	पितामहः
creator	धातृ (m.)
cried out	अक्रोशत्
cried; wailed	अरोदत्

cries out	क्रोशति
cries; wails	रोदति
crossed	अतरत्
crosses	तरति
curse	शापः
cursed	शप्त॰
cut	छिन्न॰

D

Daśaratha	दशरथः
daughter	कन्या
dead	मृत॰
deer	मृगः
demon	राक्षसः
demoness	राक्षसी
desire	कामः
(he) desires, wants	इच्छति
(having) desired, wanted	इष्ट्वा
destroyed	अनाशयत्
destroys	नाशयति
Dhṛtarāṣtra	धृतराष्ट्रः
(they pl.) did, made	अकुर्वन्
did, made	अकरोत्
(will) do, make	करिष्यति
does, makes	करोति
(you) do	करोषि
done, made	कृत॰
(is) done	क्रियते

(having) done, made, put on	कृत्वा
dog	कुक्कुरः
door	द्वारम्
drank	अपिबत्
drink!	पिब (sg.), पिबत (pl.)
drinks	पिबति
drunk	पीत॰
(is) drunk	पीयते
(having) drunk	पीत्वा
dwells	वसति
dwelt	अवसत्

E

(having) eaten	खादित्वा
ear	कर्णः
earth, ground	भूमि (f.)
eat!	खाद (sg.), खादत (pl.)
eaten	खादित॰
(is) eaten	खाद्यते
eats	खादति
(will) eat	खादिष्यति
eighth	अष्टम॰
elephant	गजः
(you) embrace	परिष्वजसे
entered	प्राविशत्
(having) entered	प्रविश्य
enters	प्रविशति

even, also	अपि
everything	सर्वम्
everywhere	सर्वत्र
evil	असाधु॰, दुष्ट॰
experienced	अनुभूत॰
eye	नेत्रम्

F

face, mouth	मुखम्
fallen	पतित॰
falls	पतति
(having) fallen	पतित्वा
falls in love	स्निह्यति (+7th)
far away	दूरे
father; Janaka	जनकः, पितृ (m.)
fault	दोषः
fear	भयम्
fearless	अभय॰
fell	अपतत्
fell in love	अस्निह्यत् (+7th)
(will) find	लप्स्यते
finds	लभते
fire	अग्निः
first	प्रथम॰
fish	मत्स्यः
fisherman	धीवरः
five	पञ्च॰

flower	पुष्पम्	(will) go	गमिष्यति
flute	वंशः	god	देवः
follows	अनुगच्छति	goddess	देवी
(like a) fool	मूढवत्	goes	गच्छति
forest	वनम्,	goes down	अवगच्छति
	अरण्यम्	goes forward	प्रगच्छति
form	रूपम्	golden	सुवर्ण॰
found	अलभत	gone	गत॰
(is) found	लभ्यते	(is) gone to	गम्यते
(having) found	लब्ध्वा	(having) gone	गत्वा
freed	मुक्त॰ (+5th)	good	साधु॰
friend	मित्रम्	good! good!	साधु साधु
fruit	फलम्	grabbed, seized	गृहीत॰
		(having) grabbed	गृहीत्वा
		green	हरित॰

G

Gaṅgā	गङ्गा
garden	उद्यानम्
gave	अददात्
girl, daughter	कन्या
give!	देहि (sg.)
(having) given	दत्त्वा
(is) given	दीयते
gives	ददाति
(will) give	दास्यति
(will) give help	
	साहाय्यम् करिष्यति
go!	गच्छ (sg.), गच्छत (pl.)

grew	अवर्धत
grief	शोकः
ground, earth	
	भूमिः (f.), भूमिम् (2nd)
grows	वर्धते
(will) grow	वर्धिष्यते

H

hair	केशः
hand	हस्तः
handsome	सुन्दर॰/ -री॰

Hanumān, son of the wind	वायुपुत्रः
happiness, pleasure	सुखम्
happily	सुखेन
happy	सुखित॰
he, that	सः
heard, listened to	श्रुत॰
(having) heard	श्रुत्वा
(is) heard	श्रूयते
hears	शृणोति
heart	हृदयम्
heir apparent	युवराजः
help	साहाय्यम्
(will give) help	साहाय्यम् करिष्यति
her (2nd)	ताम्
(to) her (4th)	तस्यै
her, of her (6th)	तस्याः
here	अत्र
hidden	तिरोहित॰
him (2nd)	तम्
(by) him (3rd)	तेन
(to) him (4th)	तस्मै
his, of him (6th)	तस्य
hit	तुदित॰
(is) hit	तुद्यते
hits	तुदति
home	गृहम्
horrible	घोर॰
house	गृहम्

how?	कथम्
however, somehow	कथमपि
husband	पतिः (m.)

I

I	अहम्
I am	अस्मि
if	यदि
if ... then	यदि तर्हि
Indra	इन्द्रः
Indrajit	इन्द्रजित्
inside	अन्तः
intelligence	बुद्धिः
is	अस्ति

J

Jaṭāyu	जटायुः
Janaka	जनकः
jewel	भूषणम्
jump	प्लवनम्

K

Kabandha	कबन्धः

Karṇa	कर्णः	(will) lead	नेष्यति
Kaṁsa	कंसः	leaf-house	पर्णगृहम्
Kāliya, (a serpent demon)	कालियः	(having) left	त्यक्ता
kill!	व्यापादय	leave alone!	त्यज
(will) kill	व्यापादयिष्यति	leaves	त्यजति
kills	व्यापादयति	led	अनयत्
killed, struck	हत॰	(having) led	नीत्वा
(having) killed	हत्वा	lifted up	उदहरत्
king	नृपः	lifts, lifts up	उद्धरति
kingdom	राज्यम्	like, as if	इव
Kubera (the god of wealth)	कुबेरः	like a fool	मूढवत्
Kuntī	कुन्ती	like Rāma	रामवत्
Kṛṣṇa	कृष्णः	likewise; thus	एवम्
Kaikeyī	कैकेयी	limitless	अनन्त॰
Kausalyā	कौसल्या	lion	सिंहः
		listen!	शृणु (sg.), शृणुत (pl.)
		listened	अशृणोत्
		listened to	श्रुत॰

L

		listens	शृणोति
		lives	जीवति
		(having) lived	जीवित्वा
Lakṣmaṇa	लक्ष्मणः	lives, dwells	वसति
Laṅkā, (Rāvaṇa's island)	लङ्का	long	दीर्घ॰
lady	नारी	long ago	पुरा
large	विशाल॰	(for a) long time	बहुकालम्
laughed	अहसत्	Lord, the	हरिः (m.)
laughs	हसति		
leads	नयति		

155

M

made, did	अकरोत्
(they pl.) made, did	अकुर्वन्
Mādrī	माद्री
magic	माया
made, done	कृत॰
(will) make, do	करिष्यति
makes, does	करोति
(having) made, done	कृत्वा
man	नरः
mantra	मन्त्रः
many, much	बहु॰
Mārīca	मारीचः
marriage	विवाहः
(having) married	परिणीय
marries	परिनयति
me (2nd)	माम्
(by) me	मया
(for) me	मह्यम्
(in) me	मयि
meets	मिलति (+ 3rd)
messenger	दूतः
met	अमिलत् (+ 3rd)
(having) met	मिलित्वा
(in the) middle of	मध्ये (+ 6th)
Mithilā	मिथिला
monk	मुनिजनः

monkey	कपिः, वानरः
moon	चन्द्रः
mother	जननी, मातृ (f.)
mountain	अचलः
mouth, face	आस्यम्, मुखम्
much, many	बहु॰
my, of me	मम

N

Nakula	नकुलः
name, by name	नाम
Nārada, a sage	नारदः
near	समीपे (+6th)
never	न कदा अपि
Nīla, a monkey architect	नीलः
nose	नासिका
not	न
now	इदानीम्
no one	न कः चन (m.)
	न का चन (f.)
(in) no way	न कथम् अपि
nowhere	न कुत्र चित्

O

O!	

ocean	समुद्रः	proud	गर्वित॰
old	वृद्ध॰	punish!	दण्डय
O my!	अहो	pupil	शिष्यः
once, once upon a time	एकदा	pure	शुद्ध॰
one, a certain	एक॰	Pūtanā, a demoness	पूतना
only, alone (emphasises previous word)	एव	(having) put on	कृत्वा
orange	नारङ्ग॰		
other, another	अन्य॰		

Q

quickly	शीघ्रम्

P

palace	राजगृहम्
pale	पाण्डु॰
Pāṇḍu	पाण्डुः
peace	शान्तिः
person	पुरुषः
person	जनः
pillar	स्तम्भः
places, puts	स्थापयति
plays (an instrument)	वादयति
please	दयया
pleasure, happiness	सुखम्
poison	विषम्
possessing	युक्त॰ (+3rd)
prince	राजपुत्रः
protect!	रक्ष

R

rains	वर्षाः
Rāma	रामः
ran	अधावत्
Rāvaṇa	रावणः
(is) read	पठ्यते
reads	पठति
red	अरुण॰
rejoiced	अरमत
rejoices	रमते
(having) replied	प्रत्युद्य
replies, answers	प्रतिवदति
ring	अङ्गुलीयम्
river	नदी
road	मार्गः

157

rock	शिला	(having) seen	दृष्ट्वा
rope	सूत्रम्	sees	पश्यति
run! (imperative sing.)	धाव	seized, grabbed	गृहीत॰
(having) run after	अनुधाव्य	self-choice ceremony	स्वयंवरः
runs	धावति	serpent demon	कालियः
runs after	अनुधावति	(having) set alight	दग्ध्वा
		set light to	अदाहयत्
		sets light to	दाहयति

S

		seven	सप्त
		she, that	सा
sad	दुःखित॰	shines	भाति
sage	मुनिः, ऋषिः	shoots, throws	क्षिपति
Sahadeva	सहदेवः	(having) shot/thrown	क्षिप्त्वा
said, spoke	अवदत्	short	ह्रस्व॰
said, spoken	उक्त॰	silently	तूष्णीम्
(having) said, spoken	उदित्वा	sin; cheating	अधर्मः
sang	अगायत्	since ... therefore	यस्मात्...तस्मात्
Śatrughna	शत्रुघ्नः	sings	गायति
Satyavatī	सत्यवती	Sītā	सीता
saved	रक्षित॰	sits down	उपविशति
saw	अपश्यत्	Śiva	शिवः
says, speaks	वदति	Sumitrā	सुमित्रा
Śāntanu	शान्तनुः	Śūrpanakhā	शूर्पनखा
searched after	अन्वैच्छत्	sky	गगनम्
second	द्वितीय॰	small	अल्प॰
see!	पश्य (sg.), पश्यत (pl.)	smell	गन्धः
(will) see	द्रक्ष्यति	(bad) smell	दुर्गन्धः
seen	दृष्ट॰	(good) smell	सुगन्धः
(is) seen	दृश्यते	(with a) smile	सस्मितम्

158

snake	सर्पः	teacher	आचार्यः, गुरुः (m.)
soldier	सैनिकः	tells	कथयति
someone	कः चन (m.)	thank you	वन्दनम्
	का चन (f.)	that, it	तत् (n.)
something	किम् अपि (n.)	he	सः (m.)
son	पुत्रः	she	सा (f.)
soon	अचिरेण	that, him (2nd)	तम् (m.)
sound	शब्दः	(in) that, (in) him	तस्मिन्
speaks, says	वदति	then	तदा
special	विशिष्ट॰	there	तत्र
(having) spoken	उदित्वा	there is	अस्ति
(is) spoken	उद्यते	therefore	तस्मात्
stands	तिष्ठति	there was	आसीत्
star	तारका	there were	आसन्
stood	अतिष्ठत्	they two are	स्तः
stop!	उपरम	they (plural) were	आसन्
stops	उपरमति (+ 5th)	thinks	चिन्तयति
straight away	अनन्तरम्	this	एतत्
strong	प्रबल॰	(he, she) thought	अचिन्तयत्
struck, killed	हत॰	(is) thought	चिन्त्यते
Sugrīva	सुग्रीवः	those	ते
sun	सूर्यः	those (plural) (2nd masc.)	तान्
Supreme Lord, the	परमेश्वरः	(having) thought	चिन्तयित्वा
sword	खड्गः	three (fem.)	तिस्रः
		threw	अक्षिपत्

T

		throat	कण्ठः
		(having) thrown/shot	क्षिप्त्वा
		throws, shoots	क्षिपति
tail	पुच्छम्	'thus'	इति

thus; likewise	एवम्
(in) time	कालेन
together with	सह (+ 3rd)
told	अकथयत्
(is) told	कथ्यते
tormented	पीडित॰
towards (used after a 2nd-case word)	प्रति
town, city	नगरम्
tree	वृक्षः
true	सत्य॰

U

unburnt	अदग्ध॰
unhappily	दुःखेन
unhappiness	दुःखम्
us (plural, 2nd)	अस्मान्
(by) us (plural)	अस्माभिः
(for) us (plural)	अस्मभ्यम्
(from) us (plural)	अस्मत्
(in) us (plural)	अस्मासु
(of) us (plural)	अस्माकम्
us/we two	आवाम्

V

very	अतीव

Vicitravīrya	विचित्रवीर्यः
(is) victorious	जयति
Viśvāmitra	विश्वामित्रः
voice	स्वरः
vow	व्रतम्
vulture	गृध्रः
Vyāsa	व्यासः

W

wailed, cried	अरोदत्
wails, cries	रोदति
walked	अचरत्
(having) walked	चरित्वा
walks	चरति
wants, desires	इच्छति
was (he/she/it was; there was)	आसीत्
(I was)	आसम्
water	जलम्
we (plural)	वयम्
we/us two	आवाम्
went	अगच्छत्
(they plural) were	आसन्
(they two) were	आस्ताम्
(we plural) were	आस्म
(we two) were	आस्व

(you plural) were	आस्त	you (singular)	त्वम्
(you singular) were	आसीः	you (singular, 2nd)	त्वाम्
(you two) were	आस्तम्	you (plural)	यूयम्
what?	किम्	you (plural, 2nd)	युष्मान्
wheel	अक्षः	you two (1st & 2nd)	युवाम्
when	कदा	(by) you (singular)	त्वया
whenever	कदा अपि	(for) you (singular)	तुभ्यम्
where?	कुत्र	(for) you (plural)	युष्मभ्यम्
Whirlwind demon, the	चक्रवातः	(from) you (plural)	युष्मत्
who?	कः (m.), का (f.)	(from) you (singular)	त्वत्
wife	भार्या	(in) you (singular)	त्वयि
wind	वायुः	(in/of) you two	युवयोः
wine	मद्यम्	(of) you (singular)	तव
wing	पक्षः	your	तव
wise	प्राज्ञ॰	Yudhiṣṭhira	युधिष्ठिरः
wish	वरः		
with, together with	सह (+3rd)		
wood, forest	वनम्, अरण्यम्		
word	वचनम्		
world	लोकः		
writes	लिखति		

Y

Yaśodā	यशोदा
yellow	पीत॰

APPENDIX 4

Vocabulary: Sanskrit – English

This Sanskrit–English vocabulary comprises in alphabetical order all Sanskrit words, with their appropriate English renderings, used in the exercises and stories found in this volume, as well as those used in the earlier Sanskrit textbooks, 'The Stories of Krishna' and 'The Story of Rāma'.

अ		अत्यजत्	left, abandoned
अकथयत्	told	अत्र	here
अकरोत्	made, did, built	अदग्ध॰	unburnt
अकुर्वन्	they (pl.) made, did	अददात्	gave
अक्रोशत्	cried out	अदहत्	burned
अक्षः	wheel	अदाहयत्	set light to
अक्षिपत्	threw	अधर्मः	cheating, sin
अखादत्	ate	अधावत्	ran
अगच्छत्	went	अनन्त॰	limitless
अगायत्	sang	अनन्तरम्	straight away
अग्निः (m.)	fire	अनमत्	bowed
अघः	Agha, name of a demon	अनयत्	led
अङ्गुलीयम्	ring	अनाशयत्	destroyed
अचरत्	walked	अनुगच्छति	follows
अचलः	mountain	अनुधावति	runs after
अचिन्तयत्	(he/she) thought	अनुधाव्य	having run after
अचिरेण	soon	अनुभूत॰	experienced
अजयत्	conquered	अन्तः	inside
अतरत्	crossed	अन्ते	in the end
अतिष्ठत्	stood	अन्ध॰	blind
अतीव	very	अन्य॰	other, another
		अन्वैच्छत्	searched after
अतुदत्	hit	अपठत्	recited, read

162

अपतत्	fell	अमाधु॰	evil
अपश्यत्	saw	अमि	you (sing.) are
अपहृत॰	carried off	अस्ति	is
अपि	also, even	अस्थापयत्	placed, put
(न कदा अपि	never)	अस्निह्यत्	fell in love
अपिबत्	drank	अस्मत्	(from) us (plural)
अपृच्छत्	asked	अस्मभ्यम्	(for) us (plural)
अभय॰	fearless	अस्माकम्	(of) us (plural)
अभवत्	became	अस्मान्	us (plural, 2nd)
अमिलत् (+3rd)	met	अस्माभिः	(by) us (plural)
अम्बालिका	Ambālikā	अस्मासु	(in) us (plural)
अम्बा	Ambā	अस्मि	I am
अम्बिका	Ambikā	अहम्	I
अयोध्या	Ayodhyā	अहसत्	laughed
अरण्यम्	forest	अहो	O my!
अरमत	rejoiced		
अरुण॰	red		
अरोदत्	cried, wailed		

आ

अर्जुनः	Arjuna
अलभत	found
अल्प॰	small
अवगच्छति	goes down
अवदत्	said
अवर्धत	grew
अवसत्	dwelt
अशृणोत्	listened
अशोकवृक्षाः	Aśoka trees
अश्वः	horse
अष्टम॰	eighth

आगच्छ	come!
आगच्छत्	came
आगच्छति	comes
आगत॰	has come, came
आगमिष्यति	will come
आगम्य	having come
आचार्यः	teacher
आनन्दः	bliss
आनय	bring!
आनयत्	brought

आनयति	brings
आरोहति	climbs
आवयोः	(of/in) us two
आवाभ्याम्	(by/for/from) us two
आवाम्	we/us two
आसन्	(they, plural) were
आसम्	I was
आसीः	you (sing.) were
आसीत्	he/she/it/there was
आस्त	you (plural) were
आस्तम्	you two were
आस्ताम्	they two were
आस्म	we (plural) were
आस्यम्	mouth
आस्व	we two were

इ

इच्छति	he/she/it desires, wants
इति	'thus'
इदानीम्	now
इन्द्रः	Indra
इन्द्रजित्	Indrajit
इव	like, as if
इष्ट्वा	having desired, wanted

उ

उक्त॰	(was) spoken
उत्तम॰	best
उदरः	belly
उदहरत्	lifted, lifted up
उदित्वा	having said
उद्यते	is spoken
उद्यानम्	garden
उद्धरति	lifts, lifts up
उपरम	stop!
उपरमति (+5th)	stops
उपविशति	sits down
उषित्वा	having lived, dwelt

ऋ

ऋषिः	sage

ए

एक॰	one, a certain
एकदा	once, once upon a time
एतत् (n.)	this

एव	alone, only (emphasises previous word)
एवम्	thus; likewise
एषः	this (m.)
एषा (f.)	this

क

कः	who? (masc. sing.)
कंसः	Kaṃsa
कण्ठः	throat
कथम्	how?
कथम् अपि	however, somehow
कथयति	tells
कथ्यते	is told
कदा	when
कदा	when
कदा अपि	sometimes (when after न) never
कदा चित्	sometimes (when after न) never
कन्या	daughter / girl
कपिः	monkey
कबन्धः	Kabandha
करिष्यति	will do, make
करोति	does, makes, puts on
करोषि	you (sg.) make, do
कर्णः	ear; Karṇa

कर्तृ	actor, doer
का	who? (fem. sg.)
कामः	desire
कालियः	Kāliya, a serpent demon
कालेन	in time
किम्	what?
कुक्कुरः	dog
कुत्र	where?
कुत्र अपि	somewhere
कुत्र चित्	somewhere
कुन्ती	Kuntī
कुपित॰	angry
कुबेरः	Kubera, god of wealth
कृत॰	was done, made
कृत्वा	having done, having made, having put on
कृष्ण॰	black
कृष्णः	Kṛṣṇa
केशः	hair
कैकेयी	Kaikeyī
कौसल्या	Kausalyā
क्रियते	is done, made
क्रोशति	cries out
क्षिपति	throws, shoots
क्षिप्त्वा	having thrown, shot

ख

खगः	bird
खड्गः	sword
खाद	eat! (singular)
खादत	eat! (plural)
खादति	eats
खादित॰	eaten
खादिष्यति	will eat
खाद्यते	is eaten

ग

गगनम्	sky
गङ्गा	Gaṅgā
गच्छ	go! (singular)
गच्छत	go! (plural)
गच्छति	goes
गजः	elephant
गत॰	gone, is gone
गत्वा	having gone
गन्धः	a smell
गमिष्यति	will go
गम्यते	is gone to
गर्वित॰	proud
गायति	sings

गुरुः (m.)	teacher
गुहा	cave
गृध्रः	vulture
गृहम्	house
गृहीत॰	grabbed, seized
गृहीत्वा	having grabbed
गोपालः	cowherd

च

घोर॰	horrible

च

च	and
चक्रवातः	the Whirlwind demon
चन्द्रः	moon
चरति	walks
चरित्वा	having walked
चाणूरः	Cāṇūra
चापः	bow
चिन्तयति	thinks
चिन्तयित्वा	having thought
चिन्त्यते	is thought
चिबुकम्	chin

166

छ

छिन्न॰	cut

ज

जटायुः	Jaṭāyu
जनः	person
जनकः	father
जनकः	Janaka
जननी	mother
जयति	is victorious, conquers
जलम्	water
जात॰	born
जित॰	conquered
जीवति	lives
जीवित्वा	having lived

त

तत्	that / it
तत्र	there
तदा	then
तम्	that, him (2nd)
तयोः	(of/in) those two
तर्हि	then

तरति	crosses
तव	your, of you
तस्मात्	therefore
तस्मिन्	in that, in him
तस्मै	to that, to him
तस्य	his, of him
तस्याः	her, of her
तस्यै	to her
ताटका	Tāṭakā
तान्	those (many) (2nd m.)
ताम्	her (2nd)
तारका	star
तिरोहित॰	hidden
तिष्ठति	stands
तिस्रः	three (fem.)
तीरम्	bank (of a river)
तु	but
तुदति	hits
तुद्यते	is hit
तुभ्यम्	for you (sing.) (4th)
तूष्णीम्	silent
ते	those (many) (m.)
तेन	by him / by that
तौ (m.)	those two
त्यक्त॰	abandoned
त्यक्त्वा	having left
त्यज	leave alone!
त्यजति	leaves

167

त्वत्	from you (sing.)
त्वम्	you (sing.)
त्वया	by you (sing.)
त्वयि	in you (sing.)
त्वाम्	you (2nd sing.)

द

दग्ध॰	burnt
दग्ध्वा	having burnt, having set alight
दण्डय	punish!
दत्त्वा	having given
ददाति (+ 4th)	gives
दयया	please
दशरथः	Daśaratha
दहति	burns
दास्यति	will give
दाहयति	sets light to
दीयते	is given
दीर्घ॰	long
दुर्गन्धः	bad smell
दुष्ट॰	evil
दुःखम्	unhappiness
दुःखित॰	sad
दुःखेन	unhappily
दूतः	messenger
दूरम्	a long way

दूरे	far away
दृश्यते	is seen
दृष्ट॰	seen, was seen
दृष्ट्वा	having seen
देवः	a god
देवी	goddess
देहः	body
देहि	give! (sing.)
दोषः	fault
द्वारम्	door
द्वितीय॰	second
द्रक्ष्यति	will see

ध

धक्ष्यति	will burn
धर्मः	law
धातृ (m.)	creator
धावति	runs
धीवरः	fisherman
धृतराष्ट्रः	Dhṛtarāṣṭra

न

न	not
न कथम् अपि	in no way
न कदा अपि	never

न कः चित्	no one (m)
न का चित्	no one (f)
न किं चित्	nothing (n)
न कुत्र चित्	nowhere
नकुलः	Nakula
नगरम्	town, city
नत्वा	having bowed
नदी	river
नमति (+ 4th)	bows
नयति	leads
नरः	man
नव॰	new
नवनीतम्	butter
नाम	a name;
	by name
नारङ्ग॰	orange
नारदः	Nārada, a sage
नारी	lady
नाशयति	destroys
नासिका	nose
निमिषति	closes the eyes
निमिष्य	having closed the eyes
नीत्वा	having led
नील॰	blue
नीलः	Nīla (a monkey architect)
नृपः	king
नेत्रम्	eye
नेष्यति	will lead
नौका	boat

प

पक्षः	wing
पञ्च॰	five
पठति	reads, recites
पतति	falls
पतिः (m.)	husband
पतित॰	fallen
पतित्वा	having fallen
परमेश्वरः	the Supreme Lord
परिणयति	marries
परिणीय	having married
परिष्वजसे	you embrace
पर्णगृहम्	leaf-house
पशु	beast (m)
पश्य	see! (singular)
पश्यत	see! (plural)
पश्यति	sees
पाण्डवाः	the Pāṇḍavas (m.pl)
पाण्डु॰	pale
पाण्डुः	Pāṇḍu
पितामहः	the Creator
पिब	drink! (singular)
पिबत	drink! (plural)
पिबति	drinks
पीठम्	chair
पीडित॰	tormented
पीत॰	yellow; drunk

पीयते	is drunk
पुच्छम्	tail
पुत्रः	son
पुनः	again
पुनः पुनः	again and again
पुरा	long ago
पुरुषः	person
पुष्पम्	flower
पुस्तकम्	book
पूतना	Pūtanā, a demoness
पृच्छ	ask!
पृच्छति	asks
पृष्ट्वा	having asked
प्रगच्छति	goes forward
प्रति (+ 2nd)	towards
प्रतिवदति	replies
प्रत्यवदत्	replied
प्रत्युद्य	having replied
प्रथम॰	first
प्रबल॰	strong
प्रविशति	enters
प्रविश्य	having entered
प्राज्ञ॰	wise
प्रातराशः	breakfast
प्रार्थयति	asks for
प्राविशत्	entered
प्लवनम्	a jump

फ

फलम्	fruit

ब

बद्ध्वा	having bound
बध्नाति	binds
बहु॰	many, much
बहुकालम्	for a long time
बालकः	boy
बुद्धिः	intelligence
ब्रह्मास्त्रम्	the Brahmā weapon

भ

भयम्	fear
भरतः	Bharata
भर्तृ	husband
भव	be!, become! (sing.)
भवत	be!, become! (plural)
भवति	becomes
भविष्यति	will become
भाति	shines
भार्या	wife
भीत॰	afraid

भीमः	Bhīma	मिलति (+ 3rd)	meets
भीष्मः	Bhīṣma	मिलित्वा	having met
भूत्वा	having become	मुक्त° (+ 5th)	freed
भूमिम् (2nd)	ground, earth	मुखम्	mouth, face
भूमिः (f.)	ground, earth	मुनिजनः	monk, sage
भूम्याम्	on the ground	मुनिः	sage
भूषणम्	jewel	मूढवत्	like a fool
भ्रातृ	brother	मृगः	deer
		मृत°	dead
		मेघः	cloud

म

मत्	from me
मत्स्यः	fish
मद्यम्	wine
मध्ये (+6th)	in the middle of
मन्त्रः	mantra
मम	my, of me
मया	by me
मयि	in me
मह्यम्	for me
मातृ	mother
माद्री	Mādrī
माम्	me (2nd)
माया	magic
मारीचः	Mārīca
मार्गः	road
मित्रम्	friend
मिथिला	Mithilā (a city)

य

यत्र. . .तत्र	where ... there
यत्र यत्र. . .तत्र तत्र	wherever...there
यथा . . . तथा	as . . . so
यदा . . . तदा	when . . . then
यदा यदा...तदा तदा	whenever...then
यदि . . . तर्हि	if ... then
यः . . . सः	he who ... he
यशोदा	Yaśodā
यस्मात्...तस्मात्	since ... therefore
यावत्. . .तावत्	as long as ...for so long
युक्त° (+ 3rd)	possessing
युद्धम्	battle
युद्धम् करोति	fights, makes battle
युधिष्ठिरः	Yudhiṣṭhira
युवयोः	of / in you two

युवराजः	heir apparent
युवाभ्याम्	by / for / from you two
युवाम्	you two (1st or 2nd)
युष्मत्	from you (plural)
युष्मभ्यम्	for you (plural)
युष्माकम्	of you (plural)
युष्मान्	you (plural) (2nd)
युष्माभिः	by you (plural)
युष्मासु	in you (plural)
यूयम्	you (plural) (1st)

र

रक्तम्	blood
रक्ष	protect!
रक्षित॰	saved
रथः	chariot
रमणीय॰	beautiful
रमते	rejoices
राक्षसः	demon
राक्षसी	demoness
राजगृहम्	palace
राजपुत्रः	prince
राज्यम्	kingdom
रामः	Rāma
रामवत्	like Rāma

रावणः	Rāvaṇa, king of the demons
रुचिर॰	beautiful
रूपम्	form
रोदति	cries; wails

ल

लक्ष्मणः	Lakṣmaṇa
लङ्का	Laṅkā, Rāvaṇa's island
लप्स्यते	will find
लब्ध्वा	having found
लभते	finds
लभ्यते	is found
लिखति	writes
लोकः	world

व

वचनम्	word
वत्सः	calf
वदति	speaks, says
वनम्	forest
वन्दनम्	thank you
वयम्	we (plural)
वरः	wish

वर्णः	colour		व्यासः	Vyāsa
वर्धते	grows		व्रतम्	vow
वर्धिष्यते	will grow			
वर्षाः	rains			
वंशः	flute		**श**	
वसति	dwells			
वादयति	plays (an instrument)		शत्रुघ्नः	Śatrughna
वानरः	monkey		शप्त॰	cursed
वायुः	wind		शब्दः	sound, voice
वायुपुत्रः	Hanumān, son of the wind		शरः	arrow
			शान्तनुः	Śāntanu
विवाहः	marriage		शान्तिः	peace
विचित्रवीर्यः	Vicitravīrya		शापः	curse
विषम्	poison		शिला	rock
विशाल॰	large		शिवः	Śiva
विशिष्ट॰	special		शिष्यः	pupil
विश्वामित्रः	Viśvāmitra		शीघ्रम्	quickly
विसर्गः	a release of the breath, shown by ः, as in रामः		शुद्ध॰	pure
			शूर्पनखा	Śūrpanakhā
विस्मित॰	amazed		शृणु	listen! (singular)
वीर॰	brave		शृणुत	listen! (plural)
वृक्षः	tree		शृणोति	hears
वृत॰	chosen		शोकः	grief
वृद्ध॰	old		श्री (f.)	light
व्यापादयति	kills		श्रुत॰	heard, was heard
व्यापादय	kill!		श्रुत्वा	having heard
व्यापादयिष्यति	will kill		श्रूयते	is heard
व्यापादित॰	killed, was killed			

म

सत्य॰	true
सत्यवती	Satyavatī
सन्ति	they (plural) are
संतुष्ट॰	contented
सप्त	seven
समीपे (+ 6th)	near
समुद्रः	ocean
सर्पः	snake
सर्व॰	all
सर्वत्र	everywhere
सर्वम्	all, everything
सस्मितम्	with a smile
सह (+ 3rd)	together with
सहदेवः	Sahadeva
सः	he / that
सा	she / that
साधु॰	good
साधु साधु	good! good!
साहाय्यम्	help
साहाय्यम् करिष्यति	will give help
सिंहः	lion
सीता	Sītā
सुखम्	happiness, pleasure
सुखित॰	happy

सुखेन	happily
सुगन्धः	good smell
सुग्रीवः	Sugrīva
सुन्दर॰/ -री॰	handsome, beautiful
सुमित्रा	Sumitrā
सुवर्ण॰	golden
सूत्रम्	rope, string
सूर्यः	sun
सेतुः	causeway
सेना	army
सोदरः	brother
सैनिकः	soldier
स्तनः	breast
स्तम्भः	pillar
स्तः	they two are
स्थ	you (plural) are
स्थः	you two are
स्थापयति	places
स्निह्यति (+7th)	falls in love
स्म	[makes a present verb into a past]
स्मः	we (plural) are
स्वयंवरः	self-choice ceremony
स्वरः	voice
स्वः	we two are

ह

हत॰	killed
हत्वा	having killed
हरित॰	green
हरिः (m.)	the Lord
हसति	laughs
हस्तः	hand
हा हा	alas! alas!
हृदयम्	heart
हे	O!
ह्रस्व॰	short

Seven Sanskrit Coursebooks for Beginners

The first group of books entitled **Sanskrit is Fun** (Parts I-III) introduce the learners to the *Devanagari* alphabets, grouping the letters according to their place of articulation, called 'Family', which comprises both the vowels and consonants.

Learners are first taught how to draw the letters. Learning and teaching is also helped by the humorous presentation of the letters in the form of animals figures. The next step is to add vowel to the consonants, and then to teach joint (compound) consonants. Finally words and sentences are formed.

Pages: viii, 76

Pages: viii, 76

Pages: viii, 60

ISBN: 978-81-208-3545-0 Pt. I (Paper)
ISBN: 978-81-208-3590-0 (Spiral Bound)
ISBN: 978-81-208-3546-7 Pt. II (Paper)
ISBN: 978-81-208-3591-7 (Spiral Bound)

ISBN: 978-81-208-3547-4 Pt. III (Paper)
ISBN: 978-81-208-3592-4 (Spiral Bound)
ISBN: 978-81-208-3597-9 (3 Pts. Cloth Set)

Pages: xiv, 162

Pages: xv, 189

The second group of books seek to teach Sanskrit with reference to the age-old stories of Krishna and Rama. **The Stories of Krishna** (Parts I-II) cover full declensions of the most common type of masculine, feminine and neuter nouns: conjugations of a simple verb in the present, future and past tenses and twelve stories based on the childhood of Krishna.

ISBN: 978-81-208-3548-1 Pt. I (Paper)
ISBN: 978-81-208-3593-1 (Spiral Bound)
ISBN: 978-81-208-3549-8 Pt. II (Paper)
ISBN: 978-81-208-3594-8 (Spiral Bound)
ISBN: 978-81-208-3598-6 (2 Pts. Cloth Set)

The Story of Rama books (Parts I – II) together relate, in 16 episodes, the story of the Ramayana. Part I introduces : the standard method of transliteration; the gerund ('having done something'); and the declension of the Sanskrit word for 'that' in all three genders. Part II covers an introduction to the imperative mood; other important noun and pronoun declensions; 'having done something' used with prefixes; the past passive participle; the conjugation of the middle voice and the verb 'to be' in present, future and past tenses; and the completion of the standard method of transliteration.

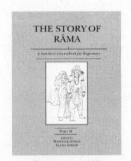

Pages: xviii, 125

Pages: xiv, 137

ISBN: 978-81-208-3550-4 Pt. I (Paper)
ISBN: 978-81-208-3595-5 (Spiral Bound)
ISBN: 978-81-208-3551-1 Pt. II (Paper)

ISBN: 978-81-208-3596-2 (Spiral Bound)
ISBN: 978-81-208-3599-3 (2 Pts. Cloth Set)